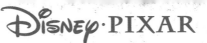

DISNEY·PIXAR

MONSTERS, INC.

SCARY STORIES

MONSTERS, INC.: THE STORY OF THE MOVIE IN COMICS

Adaptation: **Charles Bazaldua**

Layouts: **Claudio Sciarrone**

Pencils: **Elisabetta Melaranci & Anna Merli**

Inks: **Davide Zannetti & Sonia Matrone**

Color: **Mara Damiani & Elena M. Naggi**

Cover Pencils: **Lori Tyminski**

Cover Paint: **Adrienne Brown**

Many Thanks To **Dario Calabria, Flavia Scuderi & Gianluca Barone**

MONSTERS, INC.: THE HUMANWEEN PARTY

Writer: **Alessandro Ferrari**

Layouts: **Elisabetta Melaranci**

Tight Pencils: **Federica Salfo**

Inks: **Michela Frare**

Color: **Paco Desiato**

Artist Coordination: **Tomatofarm**

Cover Layout & Tight Pencils: **Elisabetta Melaranci**

Cover Color: **Mirka Andolfo**

MONSTERS, INC.: A PERFECT DATE

Writer: **Alessandro Ferrari**

Layouts: **Anna Merli**

Tight Pencils: **Andrea Greppi & Paolo Campinoti**

Inks: **Michela Frare**

Color: **Paco Desiato**

Artist Coordination: **Tomatofarm**

Cover Layout & Tight Pencils: **Marco Ghiglione**

Cover Color: **Massimo Rocca**

DISNEY PUBLISHING WORLDWIDE – GLOBAL MAGAZINES

Creative Director
Gianfranco Cordara

Project Supervision
Guido Frazzini (*Director, Comics Development*)

Editorial Team
Enrico Soave (*Senior Designer*), Antonella Donola (*Comics Editor*),
Jann Jones (*Comics Editor*), Virpi Korhonen (*Editorial Supervisor*)

Creative Operations
Silvia Figini (*Director, Marketing, Franchise and Creative Management Publishing
EMEA – Associate Publisher Global Magazines DPW*), Camilla Vedove (*Senior
Project Manager*), Mariantonietta Galla (*Franchise Manager*), Cristina Fusetti
(*Associate Marketing Manager Digital*)

Contributors Creative Operations
Chiara Zanetti (*Digital Localization Coordinator*)

MARVEL ENTERTAINMENT

SVP of Print & Digital Publishing Sales
David Gabriel

Editor In Chief
Axel Alonso

Chief Creative Officer
Joe Quesada

Publisher
Dan Buckley

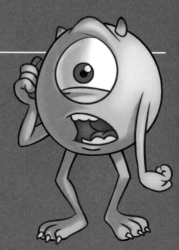

MONSTERS, INC.: SCARY STORIES. Contains material originally published in magazine form as MONSTERS, INC. #1-2, MONSTERS, INC.: THE HUMANWEEN PARTY #1 and MONSTERS, INC.: A PERFECT DATE #1. First printing 2013. ISBN# 978-0-7851-6561-3. Published by MARVEL WORLDWIDE, INC., a subsidiary of MARVEL ENTERTAINMENT, LLC. OFFICE OF PUBLICATION: 135 West 50th Street, New York, NY 10020. Copyright © 2012 and 2013 Disney/Pixar. All rights reserved. **Printed in the U.S.A.** ALAN FINE, EVP - Office of the President, Marvel Worldwide, Inc. and EVP & CMO Marvel Characters B.V.; DAN BUCKLEY, Publisher & President - Print, Animation & Digital Divisions; JOE QUESADA, Chief Creative Officer; TOM BREVOORT, SVP of Publishing; DAVID BOGART, SVP of Operations & Procurement, Publishing; C.B. CEBULSKI, SVP of Creator & Content Development; DAVID GABRIEL, SVP of Print & Digital Publishing Sales; JIM O'KEEFE, VP of Operations & Logistics; DAN CARR, Executive Director of Publishing Technology; SUSAN CRESPI, Editorial Operations Manager; ALEX MORALES, Publishing Operations Manager; STAN LEE, Chairman Emeritus. For information regarding advertising in Marvel Comics or on Marvel.com, please contact Niza Disla, Director of Marvel Partnerships, at ndisla@marvel.com. For Marvel subscription inquiries, please call 800-217-9158. **Manufactured between 4/8/2013 and 5/13/2013 by SHERIDAN BOOKS, INC., CHELSEA, MI, USA.**

10 9 8 7 6 5 4 3 2 1

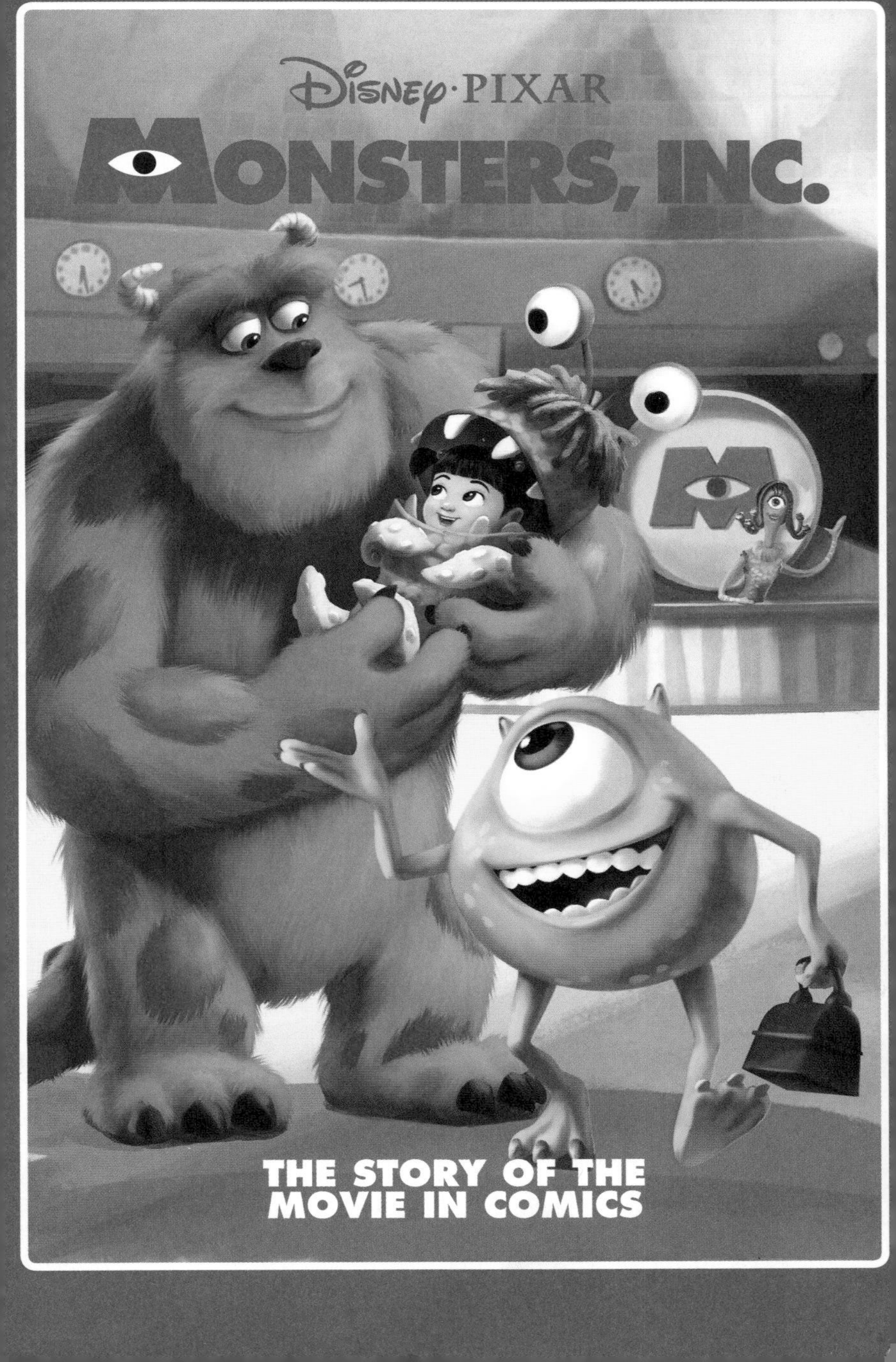
Disney·PIXAR
MONSTERS, INC.
THE STORY OF THE
MOVIE IN COMICS

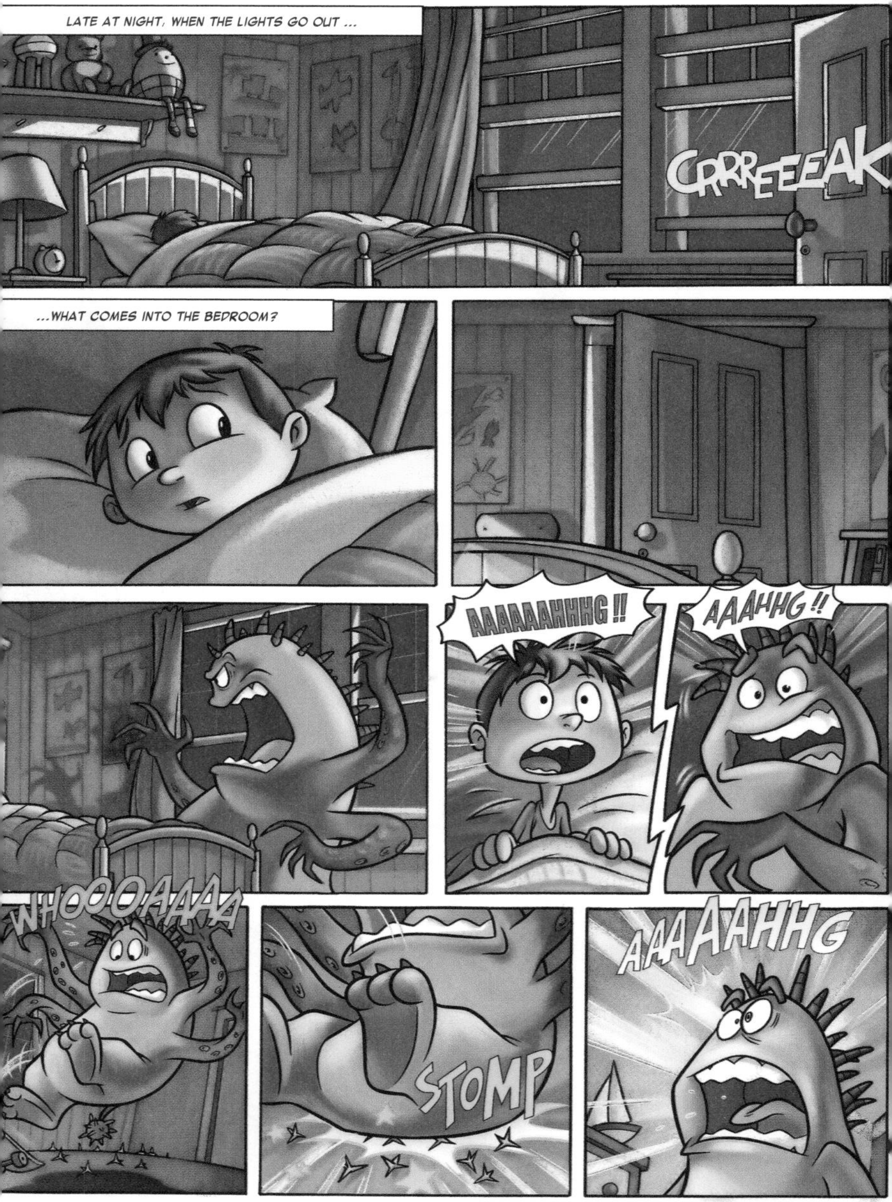
LATE AT NIGHT, WHEN THE LIGHTS GO OUT ...
CRRREEEEAK
...WHAT COMES INTO THE BEDROOM?
AAAAAAAHHHG !!
AAAHHG !!
WHOOOAAAA
STOMP
AAAAAHHG

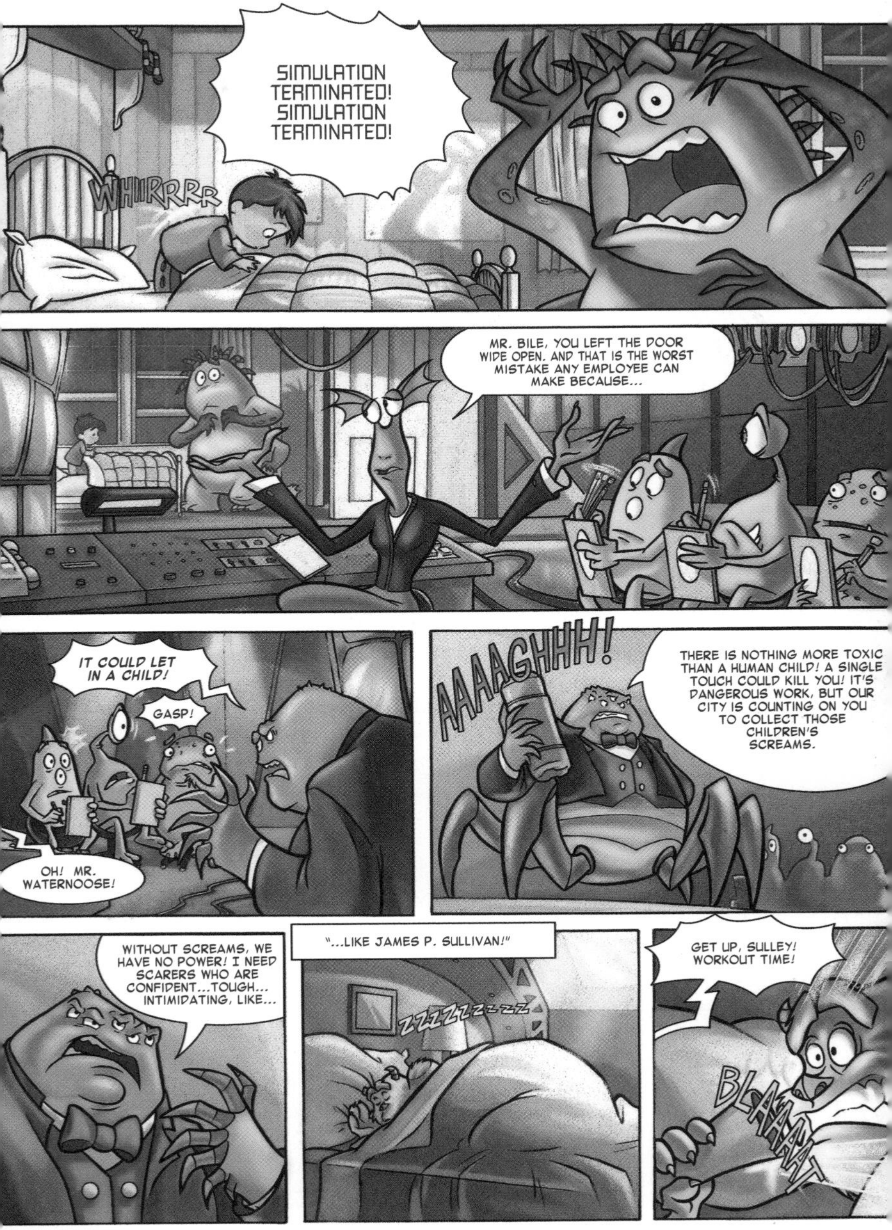
SIMULATION TERMINATED! SIMULATION TERMINATED!
WHIIRRRR
MR. BILE, YOU LEFT THE DOOR WIDE OPEN. AND THAT IS THE WORST MISTAKE ANY EMPLOYEE CAN MAKE BECAUSE...
IT COULD LET IN A CHILD!
GASP!
OH! MR. WATERNOOSE!
AAAAGHHH!
THERE IS NOTHING MORE TOXIC THAN A HUMAN CHILD! A SINGLE TOUCH COULD KILL YOU! IT'S DANGEROUS WORK, BUT OUR CITY IS COUNTING ON YOU TO COLLECT THOSE CHILDREN'S SCREAMS.
WITHOUT SCREAMS, WE HAVE NO POWER! I NEED SCARERS WHO ARE CONFIDENT...TOUGH... INTIMIDATING, LIKE...
"...LIKE JAMES P. SULLIVAN!"
ZZZZZZZZZ
GET UP, SULLEY! WORKOUT TIME!
BLAAAAT

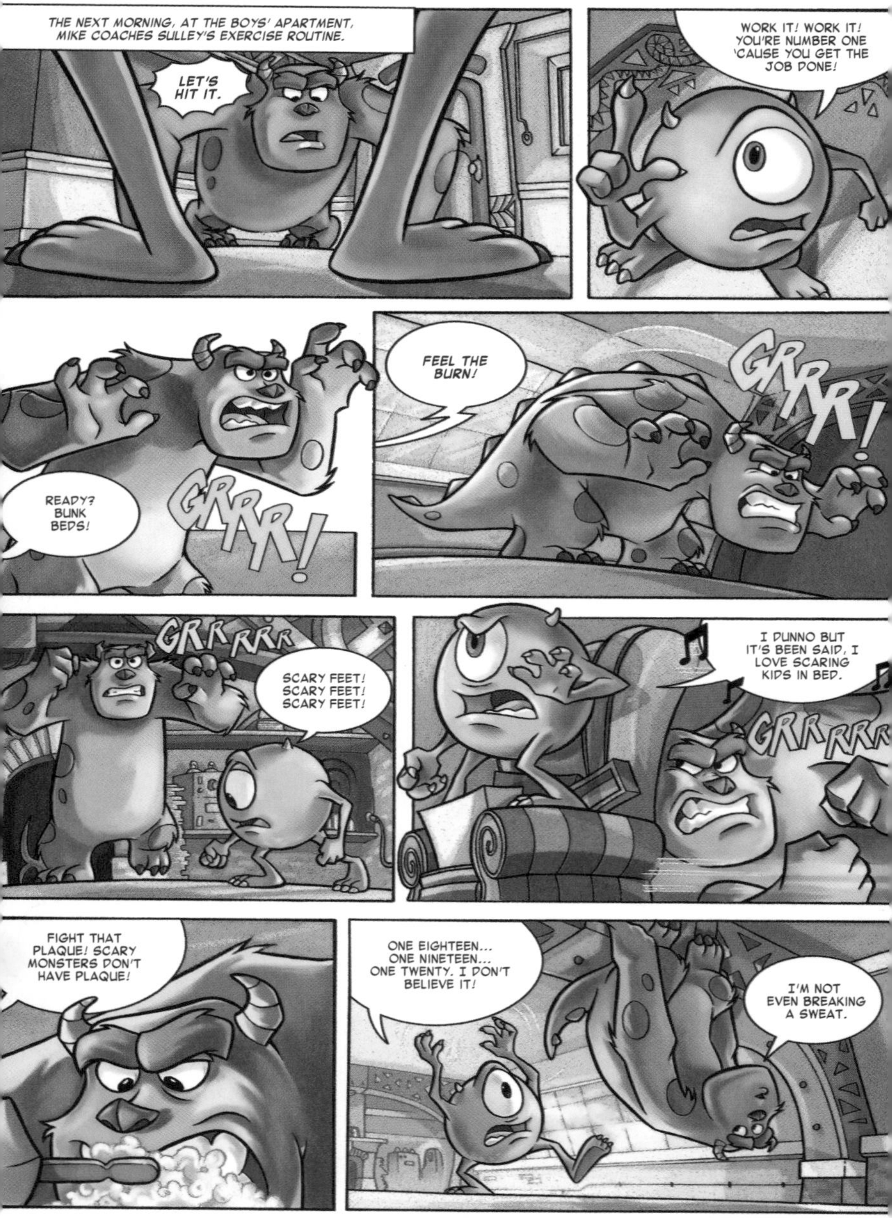
THE NEXT MORNING, AT THE BOYS' APARTMENT, MIKE COACHES SULLEY'S EXERCISE ROUTINE.
LET'S HIT IT.
WORK IT! WORK IT! YOU'RE NUMBER ONE 'CAUSE YOU GET THE JOB DONE!
READY? BUNK BEDS!
GRRRR!
FEEL THE BURN!
GRRRR!
GRRRRRR
SCARY FEET! SCARY FEET! SCARY FEET!
I DUNNO BUT IT'S BEEN SAID, I LOVE SCARING KIDS IN BED.
GRRRRRR
FIGHT THAT PLAQUE! SCARY MONSTERS DON'T HAVE PLAQUE!
ONE EIGHTEEN... ONE NINETEEN... ONE TWENTY. I DON'T BELIEVE IT!
I'M NOT EVEN BREAKING A SWEAT.

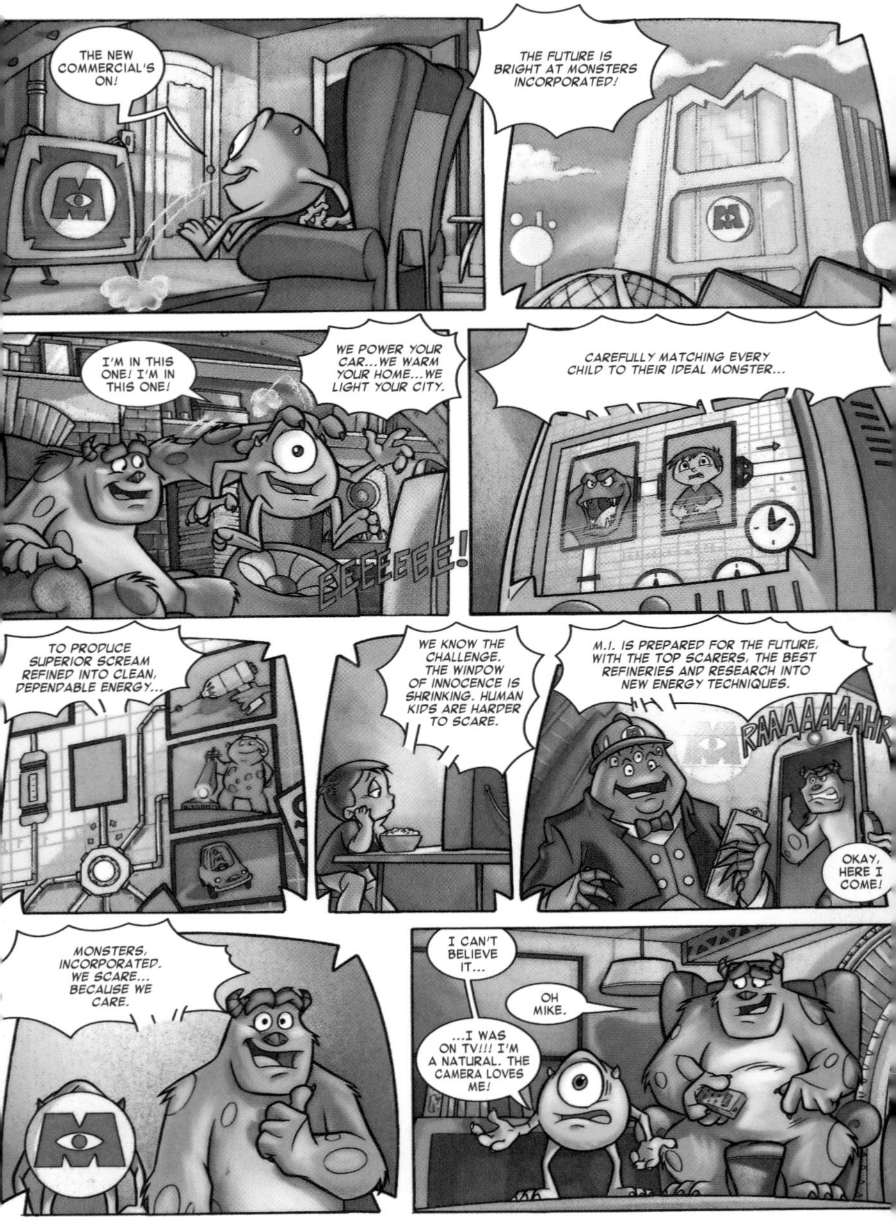

THE NEW COMMERCIAL'S ON!
THE FUTURE IS BRIGHT AT MONSTERS INCORPORATED!
I'M IN THIS ONE! I'M IN THIS ONE!
WE POWER YOUR CAR...WE WARM YOUR HOME...WE LIGHT YOUR CITY.
EEEEEEE!
CAREFULLY MATCHING EVERY CHILD TO THEIR IDEAL MONSTER...
TO PRODUCE SUPERIOR SCREAM REFINED INTO CLEAN, DEPENDABLE ENERGY...
WE KNOW THE CHALLENGE. THE WINDOW OF INNOCENCE IS SHRINKING. HUMAN KIDS ARE HARDER TO SCARE.
M.I. IS PREPARED FOR THE FUTURE, WITH THE TOP SCARERS, THE BEST REFINERIES AND RESEARCH INTO NEW ENERGY TECHNIQUES.
RAAAAAAAHR
OKAY, HERE I COME!
MONSTERS, INCORPORATED. WE SCARE... BECAUSE WE CARE.
I CAN'T BELIEVE IT...
OH MIKE.
...I WAS ON TV!!! I'M A NATURAL. THE CAMERA LOVES ME!

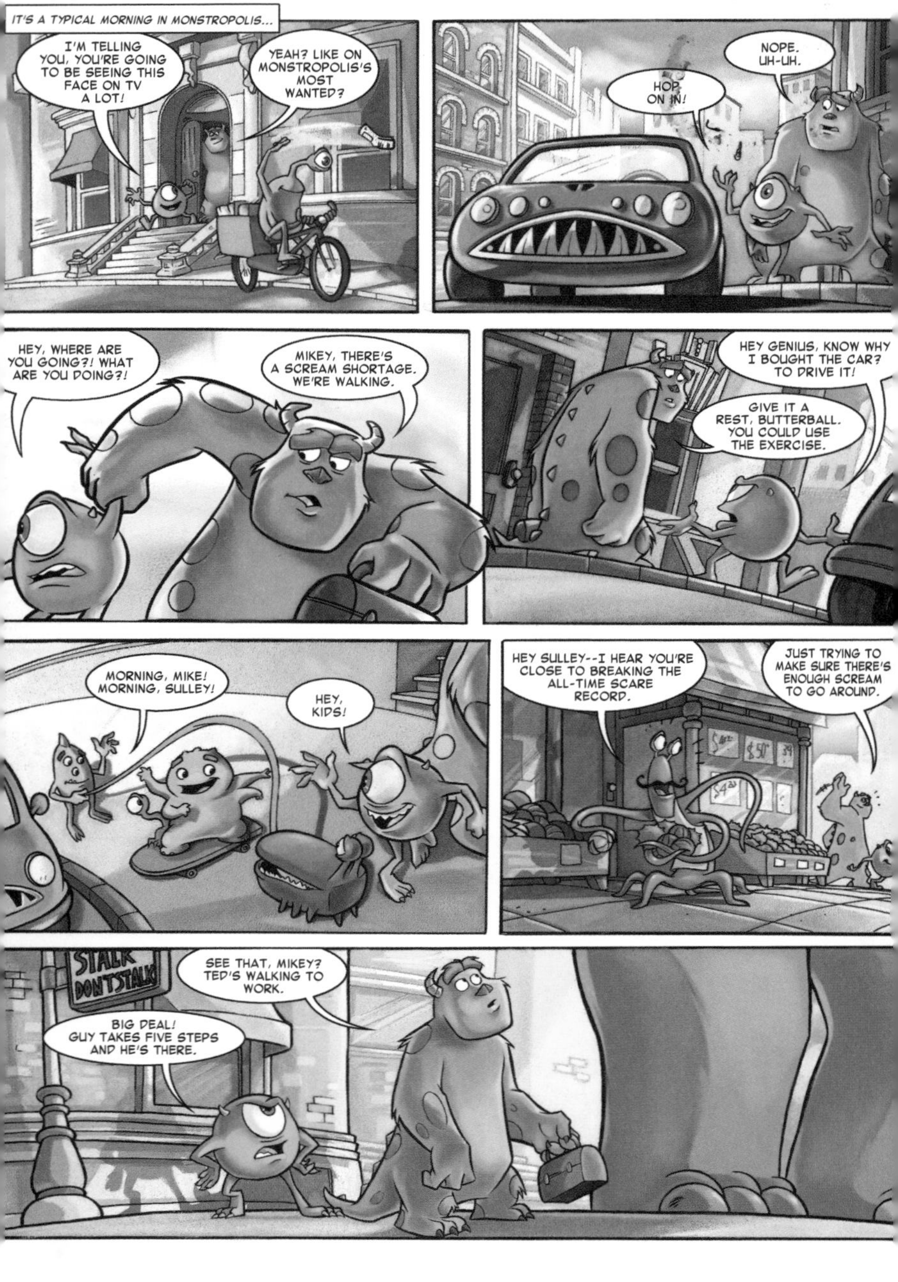
IT'S A TYPICAL MORNING IN MONSTROPOLIS...
I'M TELLING YOU, YOU'RE GOING TO BE SEEING THIS FACE ON TV A LOT!
YEAH? LIKE ON MONSTROPOLIS'S MOST WANTED?
HOP ON IN!
NOPE. UH-UH.
HEY, WHERE ARE YOU GOING?! WHAT ARE YOU DOING?!
MIKEY, THERE'S A SCREAM SHORTAGE. WE'RE WALKING.
HEY GENIUS, KNOW WHY I BOUGHT THE CAR? TO DRIVE IT!
GIVE IT A REST, BUTTERBALL. YOU COULD USE THE EXERCISE.
MORNING, MIKE! MORNING, SULLEY!
HEY, KIDS!
HEY SULLEY--I HEAR YOU'RE CLOSE TO BREAKING THE ALL-TIME SCARE RECORD.
JUST TRYING TO MAKE SURE THERE'S ENOUGH SCREAM TO GO AROUND.
STALK DON'T STALK
SEE THAT, MIKEY? TED'S WALKING TO WORK.
BIG DEAL! GUY TAKES FIVE STEPS AND HE'S THERE.

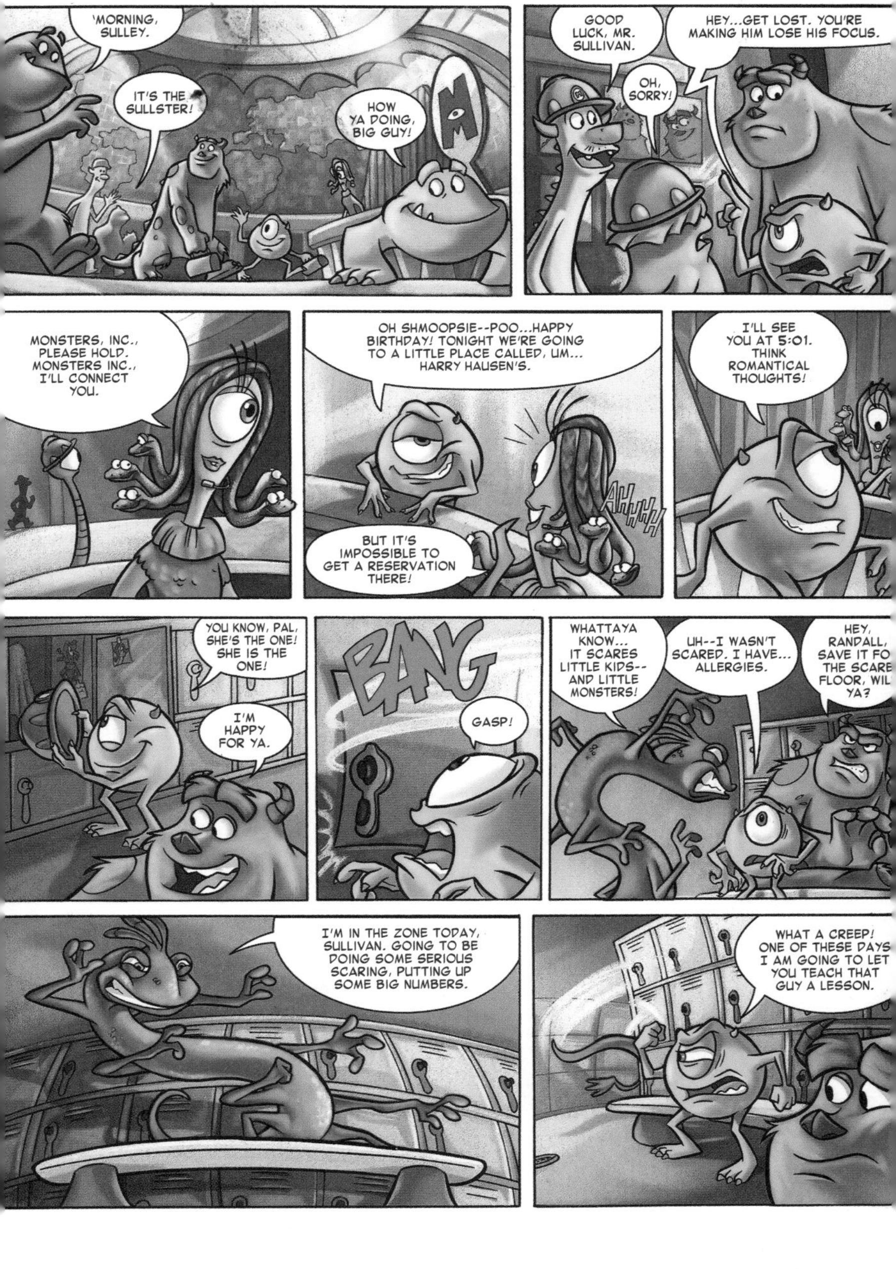
'MORNING, SULLEY.
IT'S THE SULLSTER!
HOW YA DOING, BIG GUY!
M
GOOD LUCK, MR. SULLIVAN.
HEY...GET LOST. YOU'RE MAKING HIM LOSE HIS FOCUS.
OH, SORRY!
MONSTERS, INC., PLEASE HOLD. MONSTERS INC., I'LL CONNECT YOU.
OH SHMOOPSIE--POO...HAPPY BIRTHDAY! TONIGHT WE'RE GOING TO A LITTLE PLACE CALLED, UM... HARRY HAUSEN'S.
AHHHH
BUT IT'S IMPOSSIBLE TO GET A RESERVATION THERE!
I'LL SEE YOU AT 5:01. THINK ROMANTICAL THOUGHTS!
YOU KNOW, PAL, SHE'S THE ONE! SHE IS THE ONE!
I'M HAPPY FOR YA.
BANG
GASP!
WHATTAYA KNOW... IT SCARES LITTLE KIDS-- AND LITTLE MONSTERS!
UH--I WASN'T SCARED. I HAVE... ALLERGIES.
HEY, RANDALL, SAVE IT FO THE SCARE FLOOR, WIL YA?
I'M IN THE ZONE TODAY, SULLIVAN. GOING TO BE DOING SOME SERIOUS SCARING, PUTTING UP SOME BIG NUMBERS.
WHAT A CREEP! ONE OF THESE DAYS I AM GOING TO LET YOU TEACH THAT GUY A LESSON.

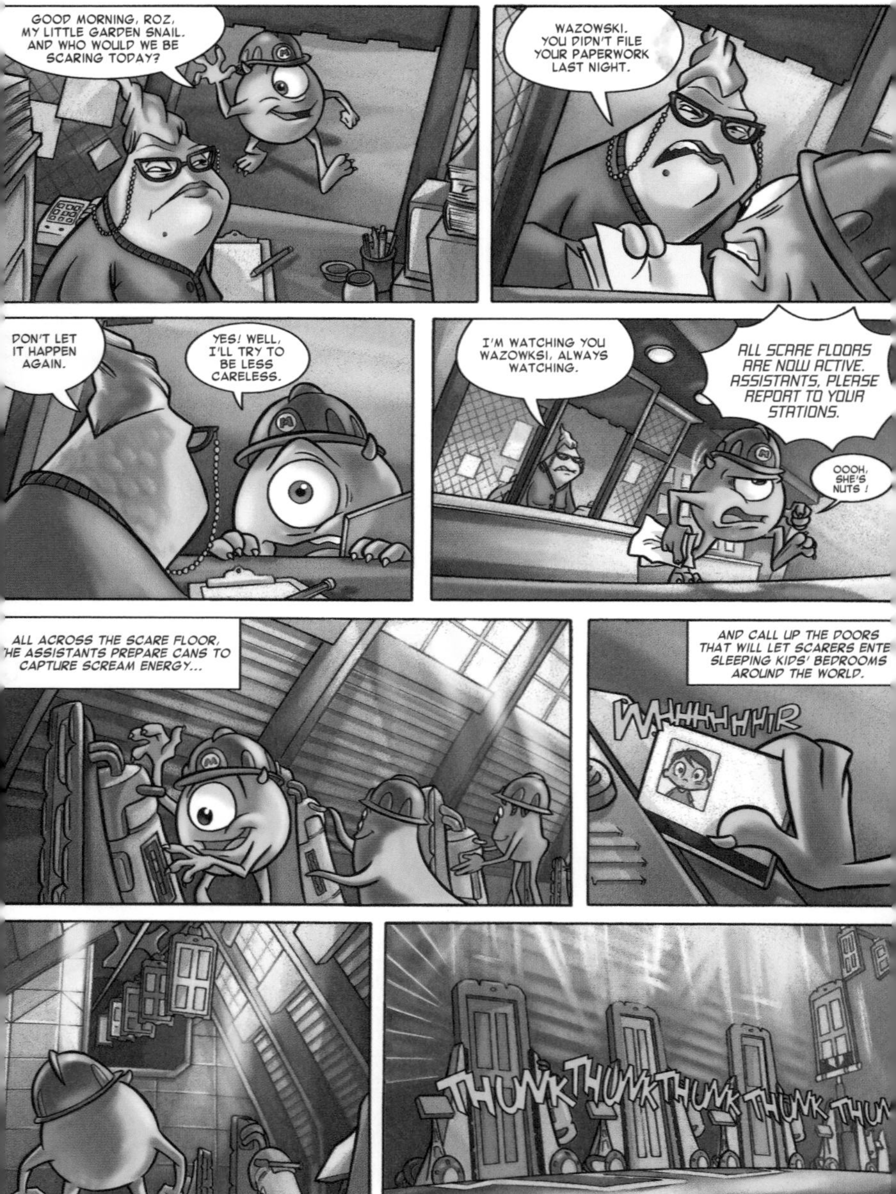

GOOD MORNING, ROZ, MY LITTLE GARDEN SNAIL. AND WHO WOULD WE BE SCARING TODAY?
WAZOWSKI. YOU DIDN'T FILE YOUR PAPERWORK LAST NIGHT.
DON'T LET IT HAPPEN AGAIN.
YES! WELL, I'LL TRY TO BE LESS CARELESS.
I'M WATCHING YOU WAZOWKSI, ALWAYS WATCHING.
ALL SCARE FLOORS ARE NOW ACTIVE. ASSISTANTS, PLEASE REPORT TO YOUR STATIONS.
OOOH, SHE'S NUTS !
ALL ACROSS THE SCARE FLOOR, THE ASSISTANTS PREPARE CANS TO CAPTURE SCREAM ENERGY...
AND CALL UP THE DOORS THAT WILL LET SCARERS ENTE SLEEPING KIDS' BEDROOMS AROUND THE WORLD.
WHHHHHHIR
THUNK THUNK THUNK THUNK THUN

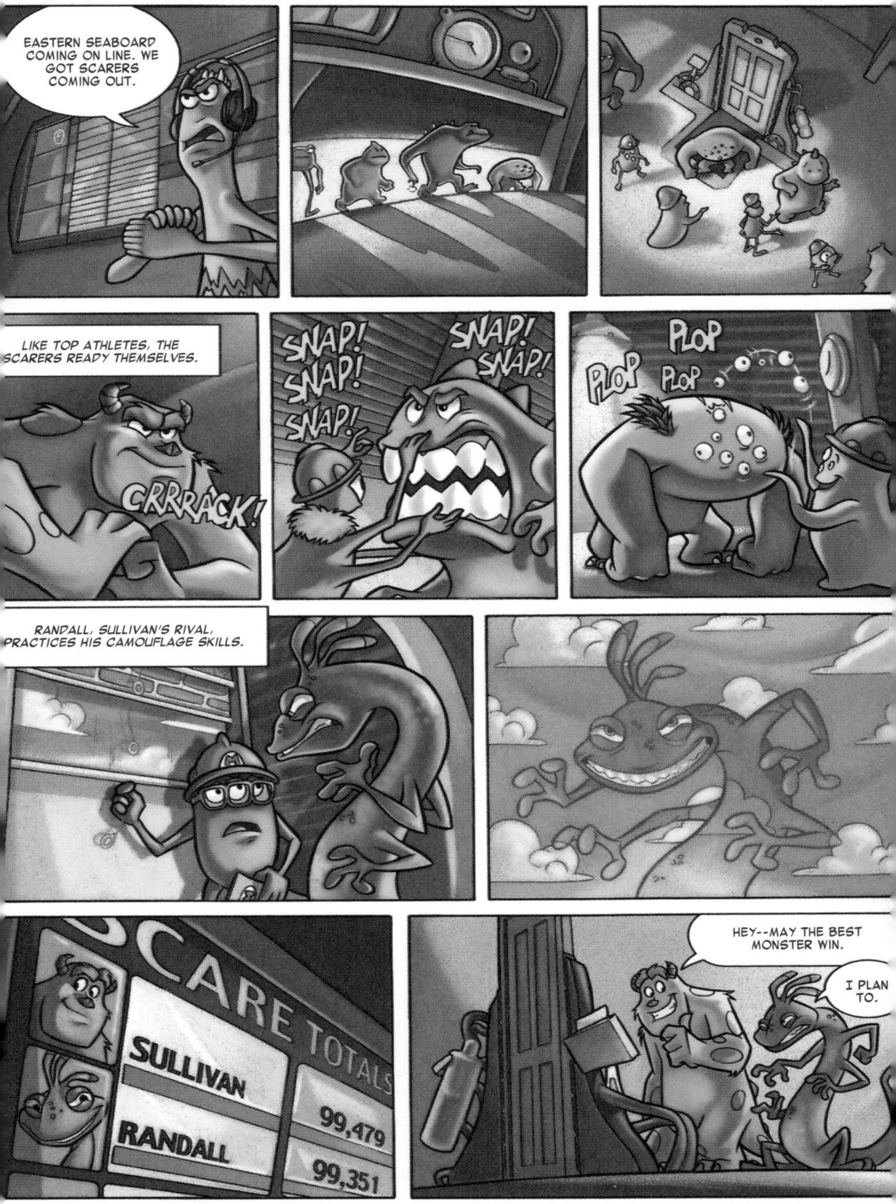
EASTERN SEABOARD COMING ON LINE. WE GOT SCARERS COMING OUT.
LIKE TOP ATHLETES, THE SCARERS READY THEMSELVES.
CRRRACK!
SNAP! SNAP! SNAP!
SNAP! SNAP!
PLOP
PLOP
PLOP
RANDALL, SULLIVAN'S RIVAL, PRACTICES HIS CAMOUFLAGE SKILLS.
SCARE TOTALS
SULLIVAN
99,479
RANDALL
99,351
HEY--MAY THE BEST MONSTER WIN.
I PLAN TO.

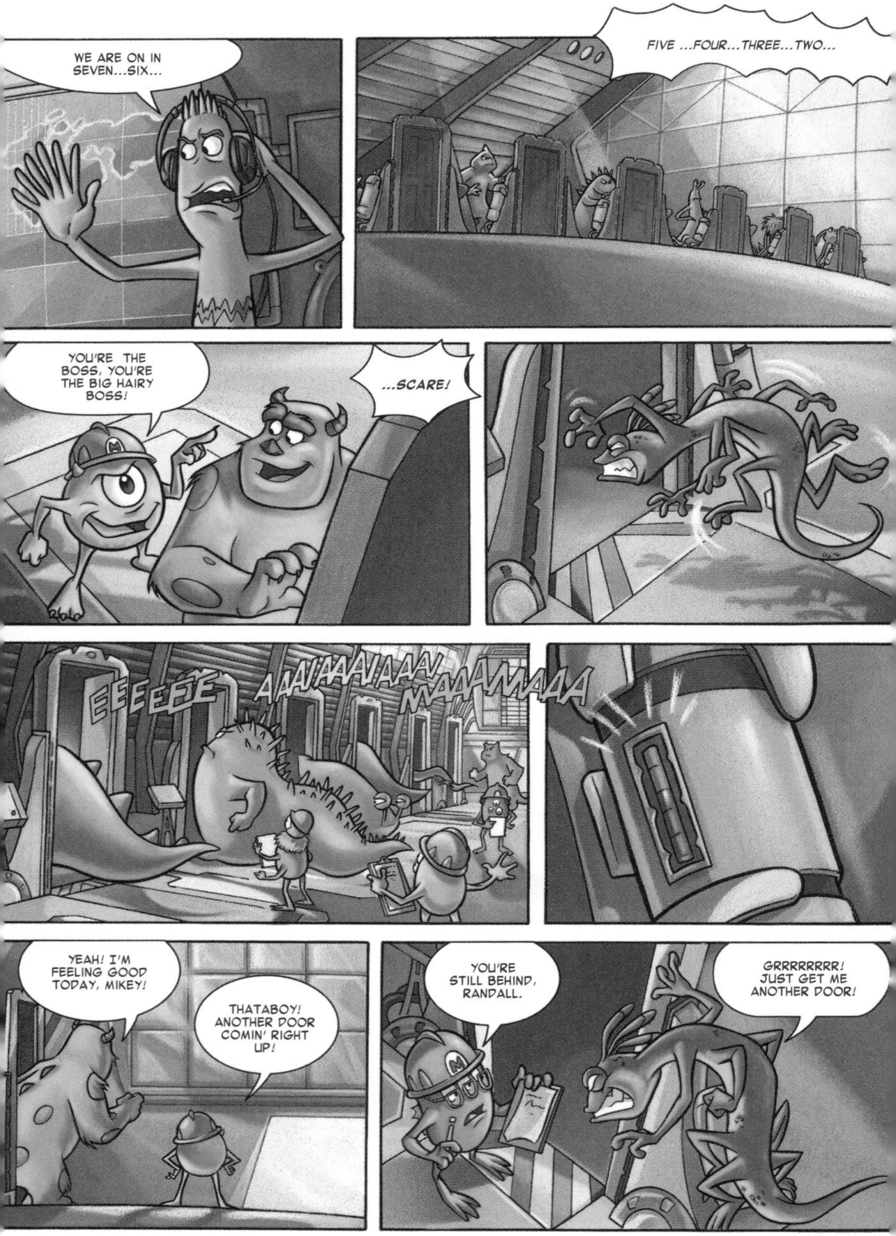
WE ARE ON IN SEVEN...SIX...
FIVE ...FOUR...THREE...TWO...
YOU'RE THE BOSS, YOU'RE THE BIG HAIRY BOSS!
...SCARE!
EEEEEE
AAAAAAAAAAAAAAAAAA
YEAH! I'M FEELING GOOD TODAY, MIKEY!
THATABOY! ANOTHER DOOR COMIN' RIGHT UP!
YOU'RE STILL BEHIND, RANDALL.
GRRRRRRRR! JUST GET ME ANOTHER DOOR!

SULLIVAN	
RANDALL	99,479
RANFT	99,351
LUCKEY	79,012
RIVERA	68,245
PETERSON	67,992
JONES	67,236
SANDERSON	66,101
PLESUSKI	58,986
SCHMIDT	55,735
PAULEY	
WARD	44,421
GERSON	41,918

WE MAY MAKE OUR QUOTA TODAY, MR. WATERNOOSE, SIR.

FIRST TIME IN A MONTH.

UH...UH...UH... THE KID ALMOST TOUCHED ME!

SHE WASN'T SCARED OF YOU? SHE WAS ONLY SIX!

I COULD'VE BEEN DEAD! I COULD'VE DIED--!

KEEP IT TOGETHER, MAN.

HEY, WE GOT A DEAD DOOR, HERE!

LOOK OUT! DOOR SHREDDER COMING THROUGH!

WE'VE LOST 58 DOORS THIS WEEK, SIR.

KIDS THESE DAYS. THEY JUST DON'T GET SCARED LIKE THEY USED TO.

SCREEEEECH

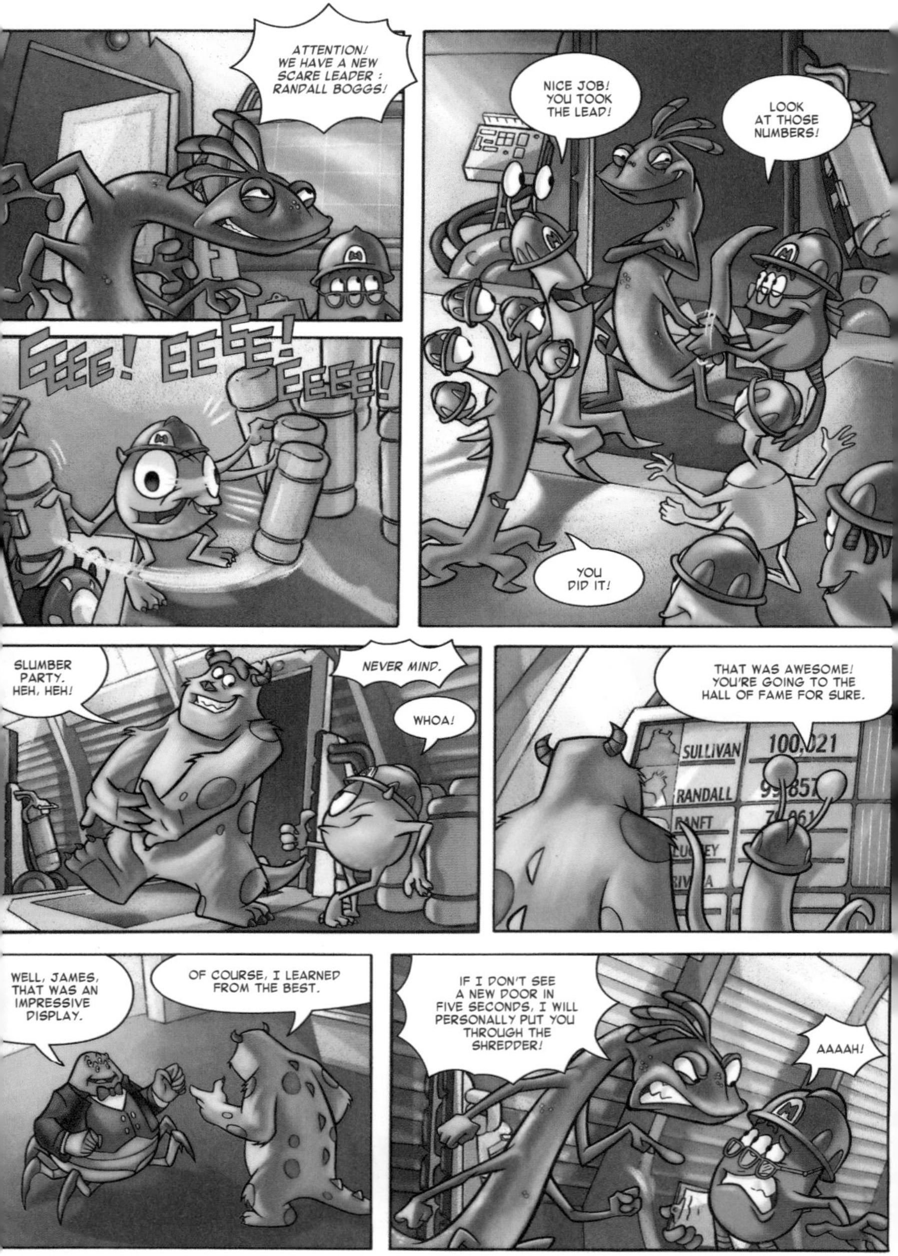
ATTENTION! WE HAVE A NEW SCARE LEADER : RANDALL BOGGS!
NICE JOB! YOU TOOK THE LEAD!
LOOK AT THOSE NUMBERS!
EEEE! EEEE! EEEE!
YOU DID IT!
SLUMBER PARTY. HEH, HEH!
NEVER MIND.
WHOA!
THAT WAS AWESOME! YOU'RE GOING TO THE HALL OF FAME FOR SURE.
SULLIVAN
100,021
RANDALL
WELL, JAMES, THAT WAS AN IMPRESSIVE DISPLAY.
OF COURSE, I LEARNED FROM THE BEST.
IF I DON'T SEE A NEW DOOR IN FIVE SECONDS, I WILL PERSONALLY PUT YOU THROUGH THE SHREDDER!
AAAAH!

SUDDENLY, DISASTER STRIKES!

KEEP THE DOORS COMIN'. I'M ON A ROLL TODAY.

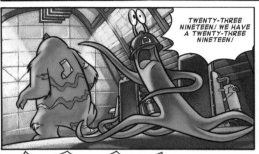

TWENTY-THREE NINETEEN! WE HAVE A TWENTY-THREE NINETEEN!

GEORGE SANDERSON, PLEASE REMAIN MOTIONLESS! PREPARE FOR DECONTAMINATION!

GET IT OFF!!

DUCK AND COVER, PEOPLE!

ALERTED TO THE DISASTER, THE DREADED C.D.A. (CHILD DETECTIVE AGEN RUSHES TO THE SCENE!

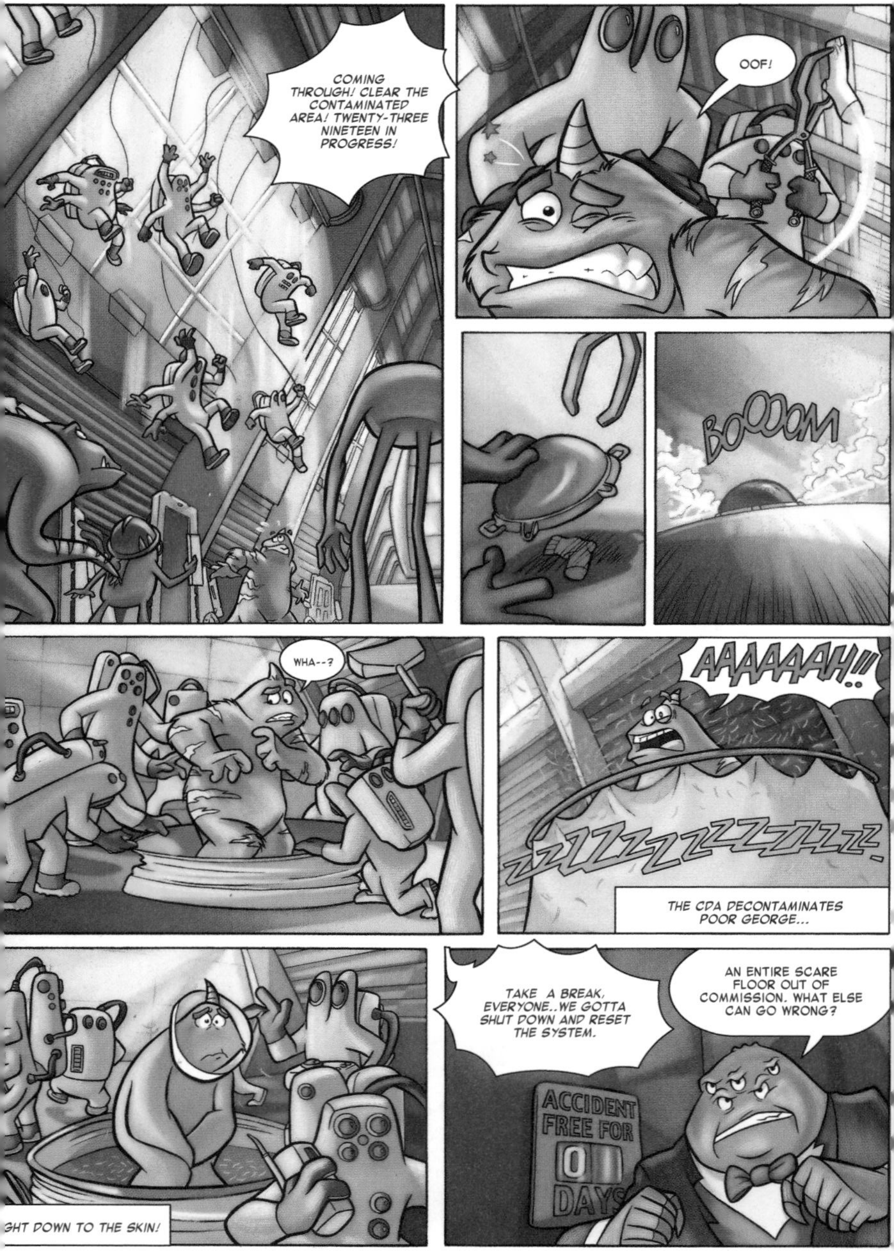

COMING THROUGH! CLEAR THE CONTAMINATED AREA! TWENTY-THREE NINETEEN IN PROGRESS!
OOF!
BOOOOM
WHA--?
AAAAAAH!!
ZZZZZZZZZZZZZZZZ-
THE CDA DECONTAMINATES POOR GEORGE...
GHT DOWN TO THE SKIN!
TAKE A BREAK, EVERYONE..WE GOTTA SHUT DOWN AND RESET THE SYSTEM.
AN ENTIRE SCARE FLOOR OUT OF COMMISSION. WHAT ELSE CAN GO WRONG?
ACCIDENT FREE FOR 0 DAYS

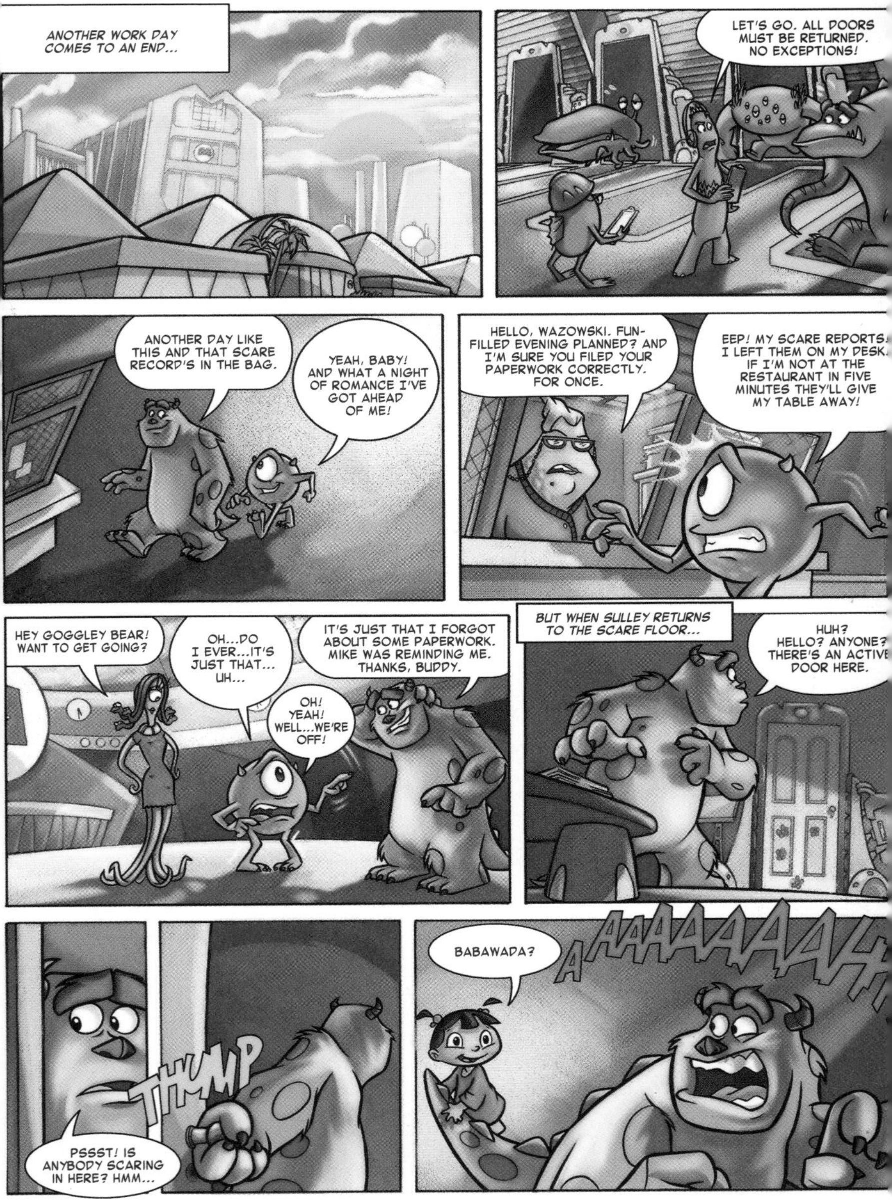
ANOTHER WORK DAY COMES TO AN END...
LET'S GO. ALL DOORS MUST BE RETURNED. NO EXCEPTIONS!
ANOTHER DAY LIKE THIS AND THAT SCARE RECORD'S IN THE BAG.
YEAH, BABY! AND WHAT A NIGHT OF ROMANCE I'VE GOT AHEAD OF ME!
HELLO, WAZOWSKI. FUN-FILLED EVENING PLANNED? AND I'M SURE YOU FILED YOUR PAPERWORK CORRECTLY. FOR ONCE.
EEP! MY SCARE REPORTS! I LEFT THEM ON MY DESK! IF I'M NOT AT THE RESTAURANT IN FIVE MINUTES THEY'LL GIVE MY TABLE AWAY!
HEY GOGGLEY BEAR! WANT TO GET GOING?
OH...DO I EVER...IT'S JUST THAT... UH...
IT'S JUST THAT I FORGOT ABOUT SOME PAPERWORK. MIKE WAS REMINDING ME. THANKS, BUDDY.
OH! YEAH! WELL...WE'RE OFF!
BUT WHEN SULLEY RETURNS TO THE SCARE FLOOR...
HUH? HELLO? ANYONE? THERE'S AN ACTIVE DOOR HERE.
THUMP
PSSST! IS ANYBODY SCARING IN HERE? HMM...
BABAWADA?
AAAAAAAAAH

SULLIVAN TRIES TO PLACE THE CHILD BACK IN HER ROOM...

AYHA!

AAAAAHH!

BUT SHE SNEAKS OUT AGAIN!

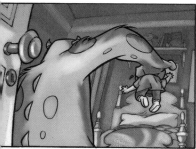

THUD

CRASH

AAAAAHH!

JUST THEN SULLEY HEARS A NOISE! SOMEONE'S COMING!

SQUEAK
SQUEAK
SQUEAK
SQUEAK

IT'S RANDALL, ON A MYSTERIOUS ERRAND!

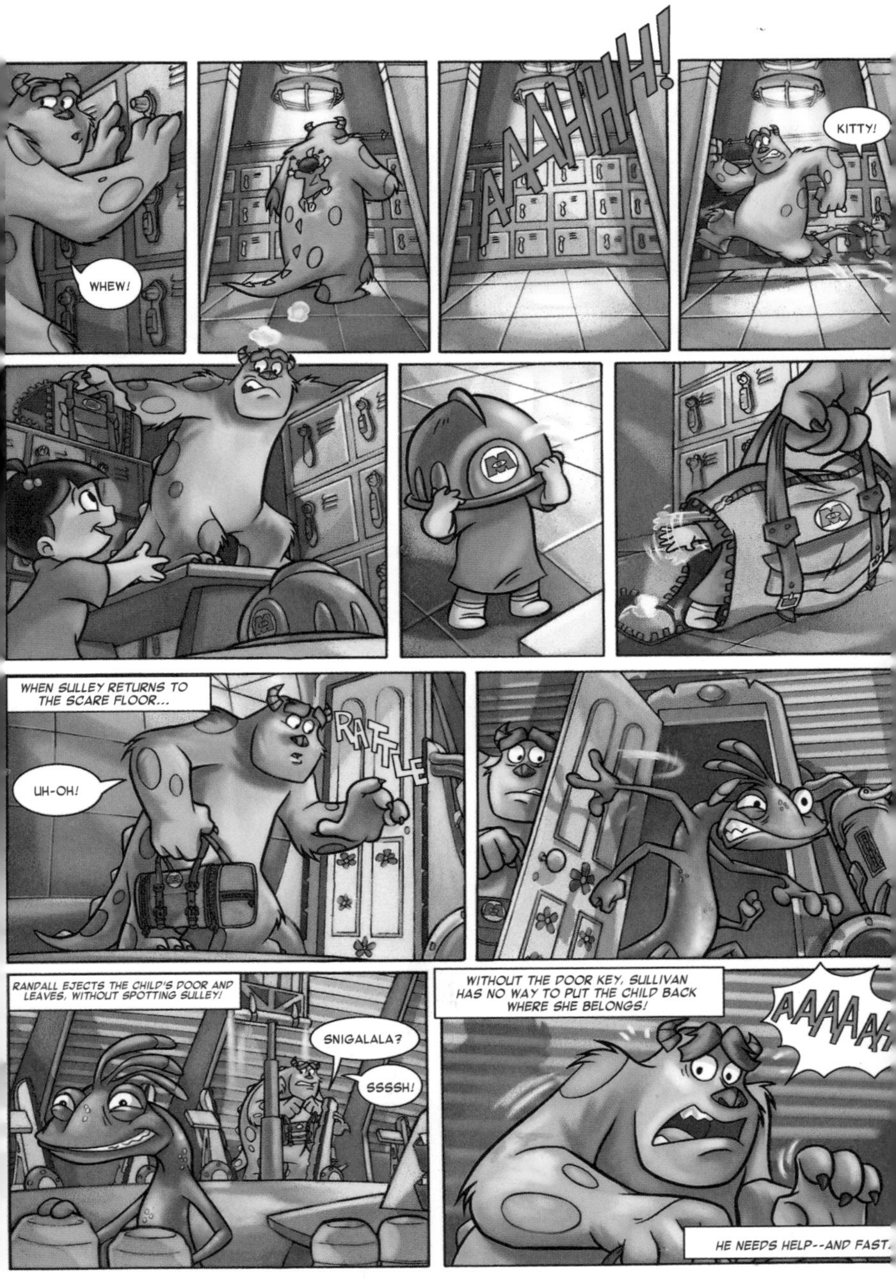
WHEW!
AAAHHH!
KITTY!
WHEN SULLEY RETURNS TO THE SCARE FLOOR...
UH-OH!
RATTLE
RANDALL EJECTS THE CHILD'S DOOR AND LEAVES, WITHOUT SPOTTING SULLEY!
SNIGALALA?
SSSSH!
WITHOUT THE DOOR KEY, SULLIVAN HAS NO WAY TO PUT THE CHILD BACK WHERE SHE BELONGS!
AAAAAAH
HE NEEDS HELP--AND FAST.

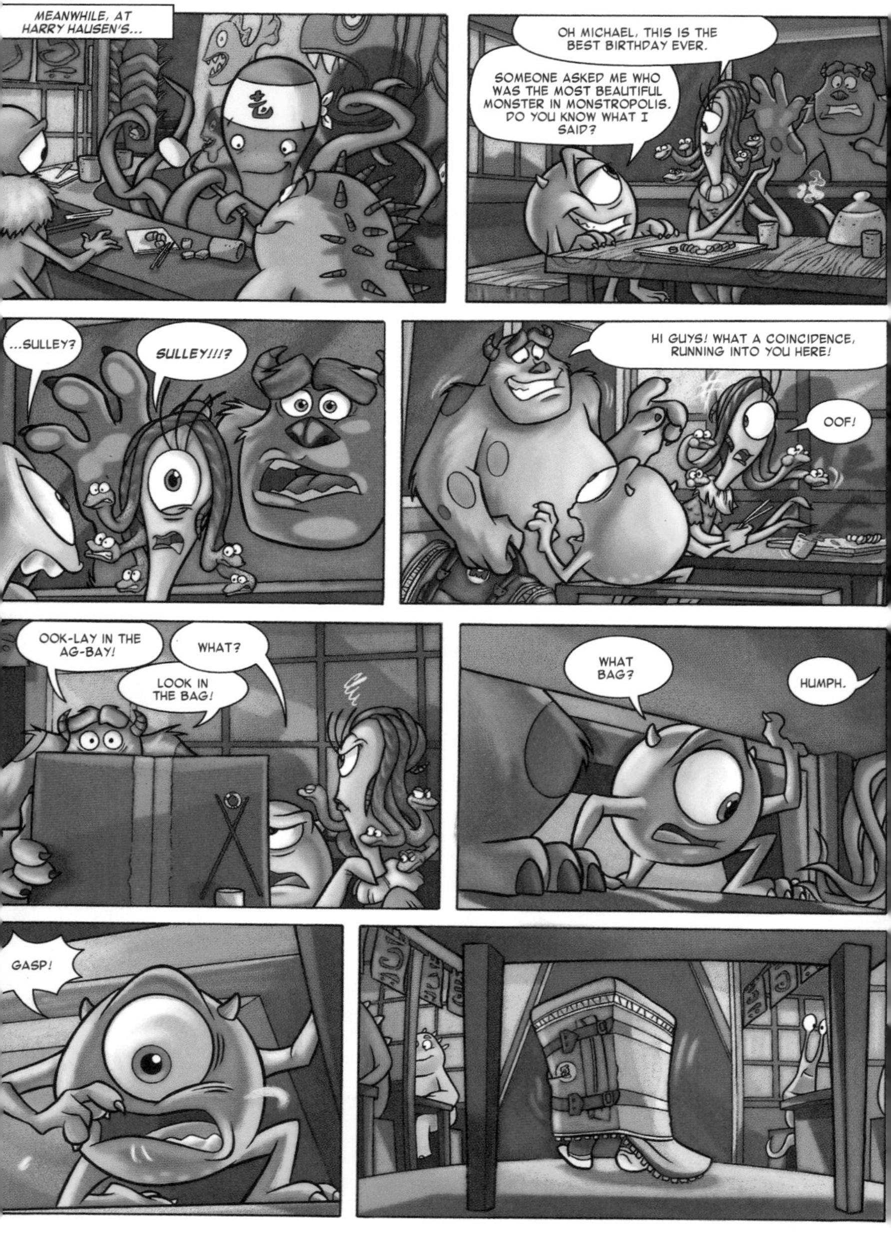
MEANWHILE, AT HARRY HAUSEN'S...
OH MICHAEL, THIS IS THE BEST BIRTHDAY EVER.
SOMEONE ASKED ME WHO WAS THE MOST BEAUTIFUL MONSTER IN MONSTROPOLIS. DO YOU KNOW WHAT I SAID?
...SULLEY?
SULLEY!!!?
HI GUYS! WHAT A COINCIDENCE, RUNNING INTO YOU HERE!
OOF!
OOK-LAY IN THE AG-BAY!
WHAT?
LOOK IN THE BAG!
WHAT BAG?
HUMPH.
GASP!

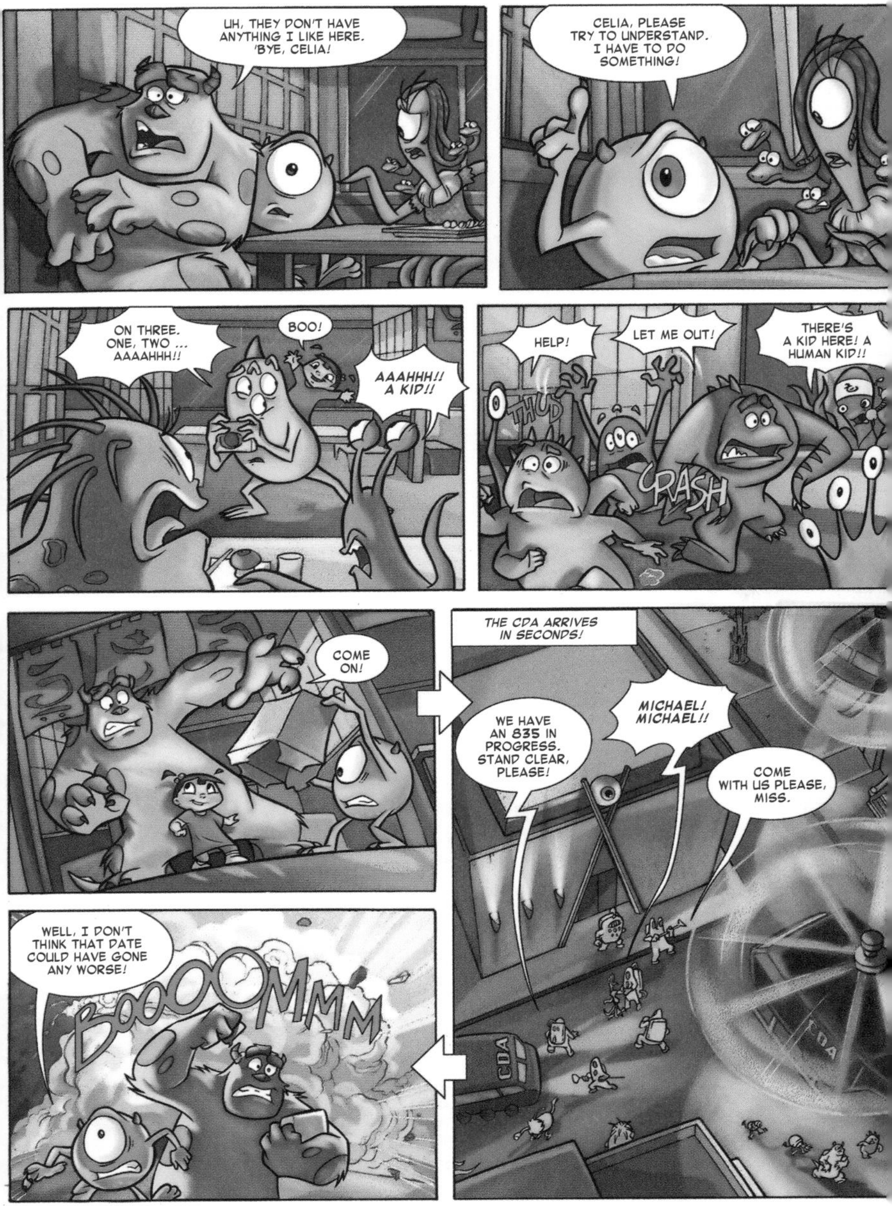
UH, THEY DON'T HAVE ANYTHING I LIKE HERE. 'BYE, CELIA!
CELIA, PLEASE TRY TO UNDERSTAND. I HAVE TO DO SOMETHING!
ON THREE. ONE, TWO ... AAAAHHH!!
BOO!
AAAHHH!! A KID!!
HELP!
LET ME OUT!
THERE'S A KID HERE! A HUMAN KID!!
THUD
CRASH
COME ON!
THE CDA ARRIVES IN SECONDS!
WE HAVE AN 835 IN PROGRESS. STAND CLEAR, PLEASE!
MICHAEL! MICHAEL!!
COME WITH US PLEASE, MISS.
CDA
WELL, I DON'T THINK THAT DATE COULD HAVE GONE ANY WORSE!
BOOOOMMMM

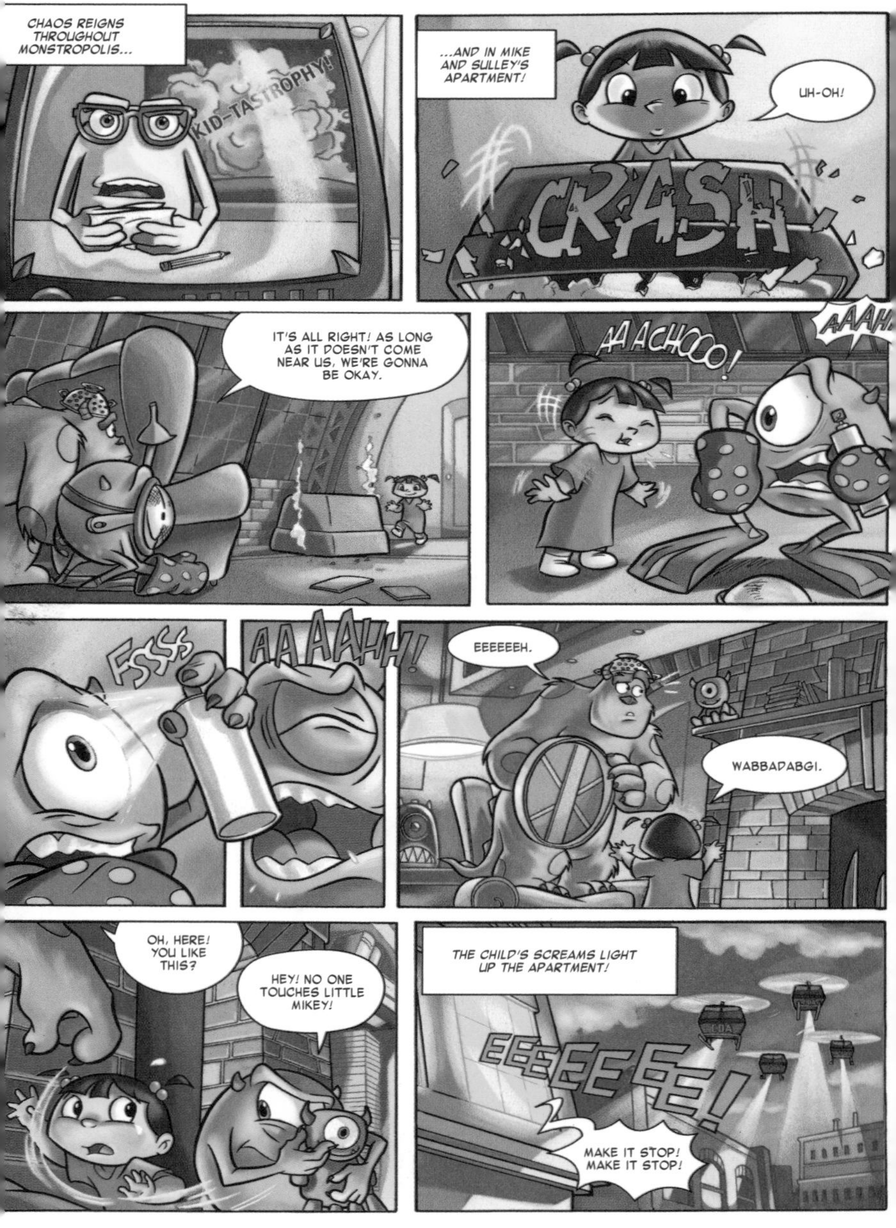
CHAOS REIGNS THROUGHOUT MONSTROPOLIS...
KID-TASTROPHY!
...AND IN MIKE AND SULLEY'S APARTMENT!
UH-OH!
CRASH
IT'S ALL RIGHT! AS LONG AS IT DOESN'T COME NEAR US, WE'RE GONNA BE OKAY.
AAACHOOO!
AAAH!
FSSSS
AAAAAHH!
EEEEEEH.
WABBADABGI.
OH, HERE! YOU LIKE THIS?
HEY! NO ONE TOUCHES LITTLE MIKEY!
THE CHILD'S SCREAMS LIGHT UP THE APARTMENT!
EEEEEEEE!
MAKE IT STOP! MAKE IT STOP!

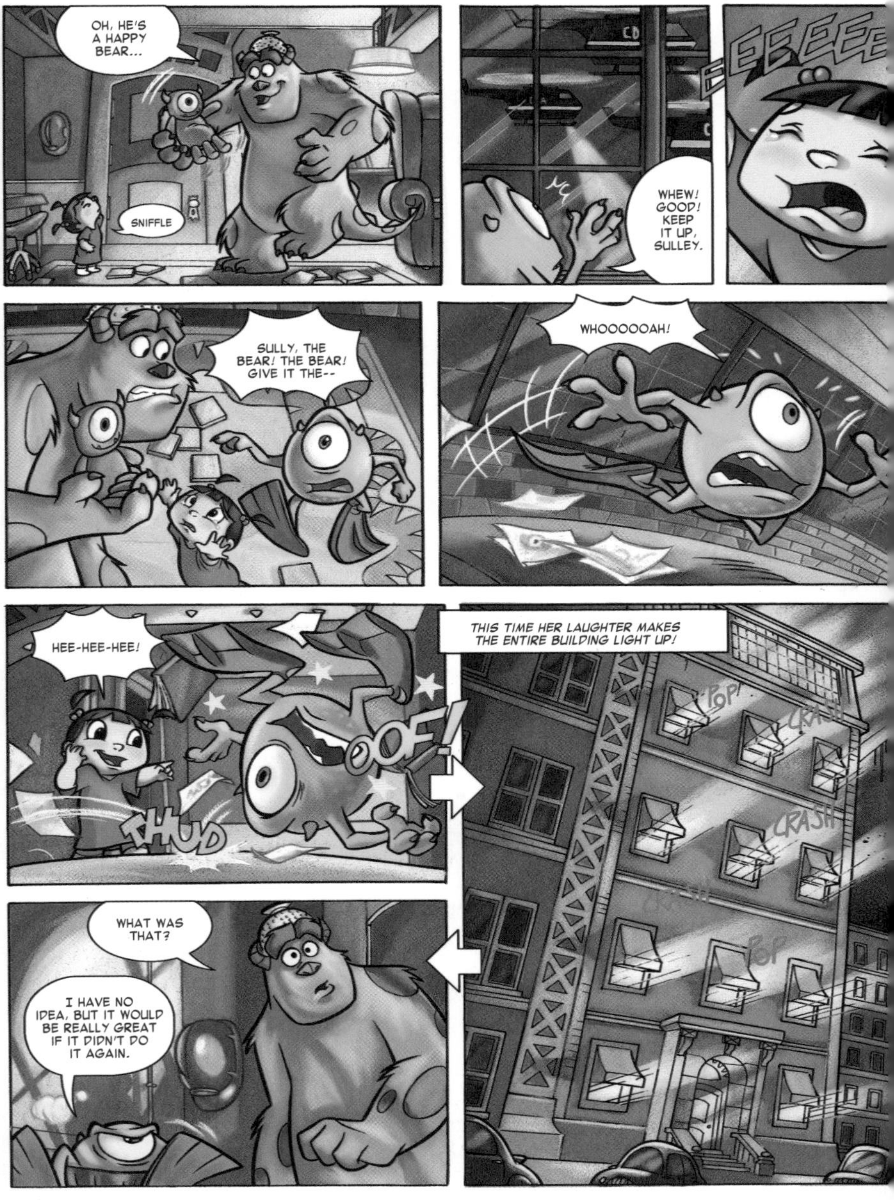
OH, HE'S A HAPPY BEAR...
SNIFFLE
WHEW! GOOD! KEEP IT UP, SULLEY.
EEEEEE
SULLY, THE BEAR! THE BEAR! GIVE IT THE--
WHOOOOOAH!
HEE-HEE-HEE!
OOF!
THUD
THIS TIME HER LAUGHTER MAKES THE ENTIRE BUILDING LIGHT UP!
POP!
CRASH
CRASH
POP
WHAT WAS THAT?
I HAVE NO IDEA, BUT IT WOULD BE REALLY GREAT IF IT DIDN'T DO IT AGAIN.

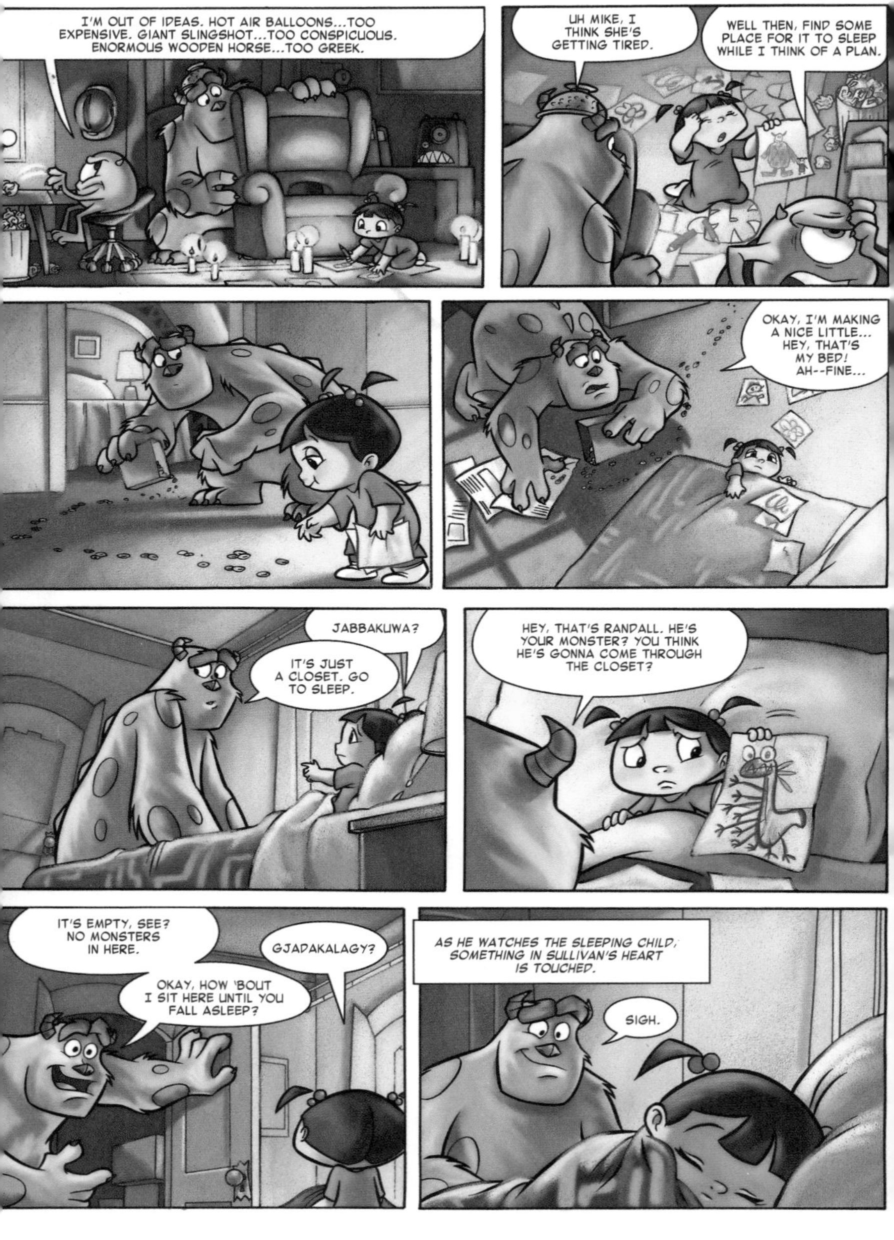
I'M OUT OF IDEAS. HOT AIR BALLOONS...TOO EXPENSIVE. GIANT SLINGSHOT...TOO CONSPICUOUS. ENORMOUS WOODEN HORSE...TOO GREEK.
UH MIKE, I THINK SHE'S GETTING TIRED.
WELL THEN, FIND SOME PLACE FOR IT TO SLEEP WHILE I THINK OF A PLAN.
OKAY, I'M MAKING A NICE LITTLE... HEY, THAT'S MY BED! AH--FINE...
JABBAKUWA?
IT'S JUST A CLOSET. GO TO SLEEP.
HEY, THAT'S RANDALL. HE'S YOUR MONSTER? YOU THINK HE'S GONNA COME THROUGH THE CLOSET?
IT'S EMPTY, SEE? NO MONSTERS IN HERE.
GJADAKALAGY?
OKAY, HOW 'BOUT I SIT HERE UNTIL YOU FALL ASLEEP?
AS HE WATCHES THE SLEEPING CHILD, SOMETHING IN SULLIVAN'S HEART IS TOUCHED.
SIGH.

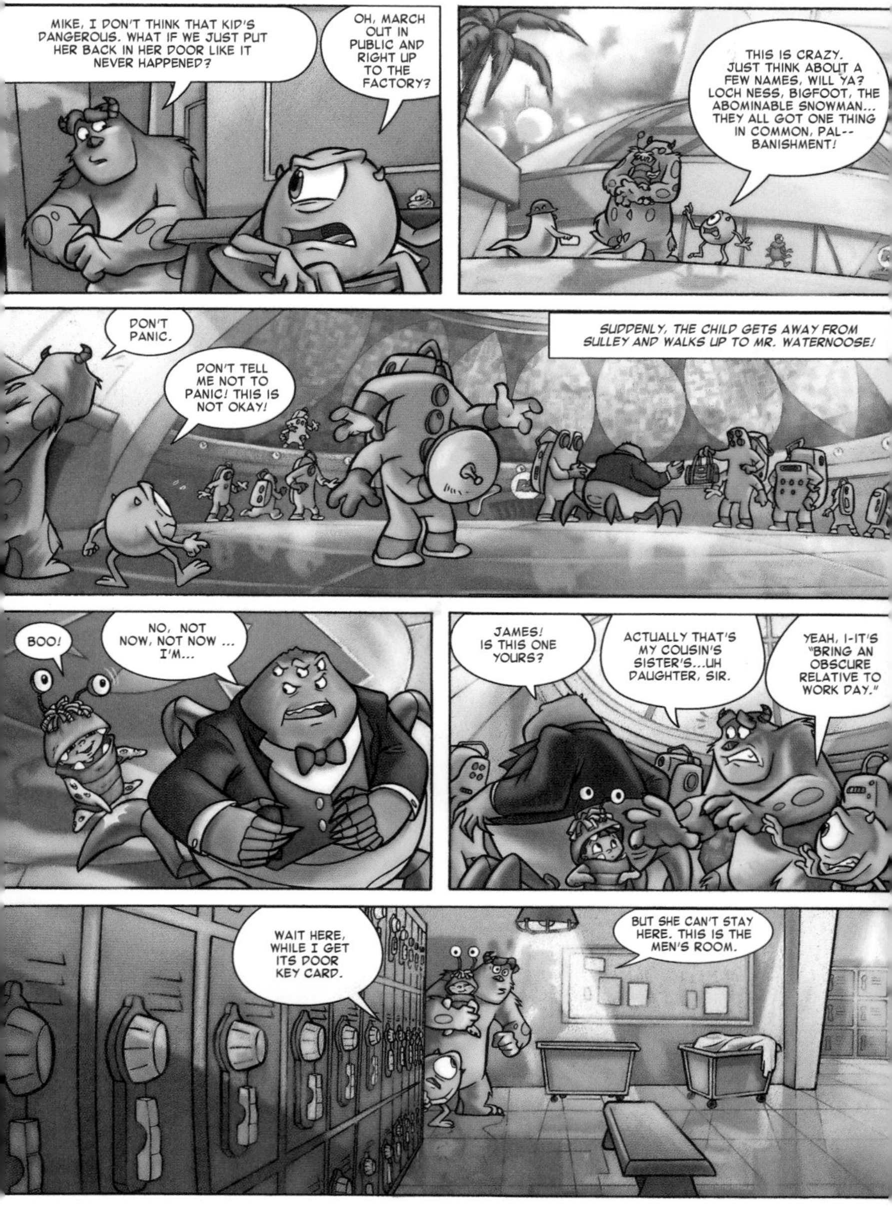
MIKE, I DON'T THINK THAT KID'S DANGEROUS. WHAT IF WE JUST PUT HER BACK IN HER DOOR LIKE IT NEVER HAPPENED?
OH, MARCH OUT IN PUBLIC AND RIGHT UP TO THE FACTORY?
THIS IS CRAZY. JUST THINK ABOUT A FEW NAMES, WILL YA? LOCH NESS, BIGFOOT, THE ABOMINABLE SNOWMAN... THEY ALL GOT ONE THING IN COMMON, PAL-- BANISHMENT!
DON'T PANIC.
DON'T TELL ME NOT TO PANIC! THIS IS NOT OKAY!
SUDDENLY, THE CHILD GETS AWAY FROM SULLEY AND WALKS UP TO MR. WATERNOOSE!
BOO!
NO, NOT NOW, NOT NOW ... I'M...
JAMES! IS THIS ONE YOURS?
ACTUALLY THAT'S MY COUSIN'S SISTER'S...UH DAUGHTER, SIR.
YEAH, I-IT'S "BRING AN OBSCURE RELATIVE TO WORK DAY."
WAIT HERE, WHILE I GET ITS DOOR KEY CARD.
BUT SHE CAN'T STAY HERE. THIS IS THE MEN'S ROOM.

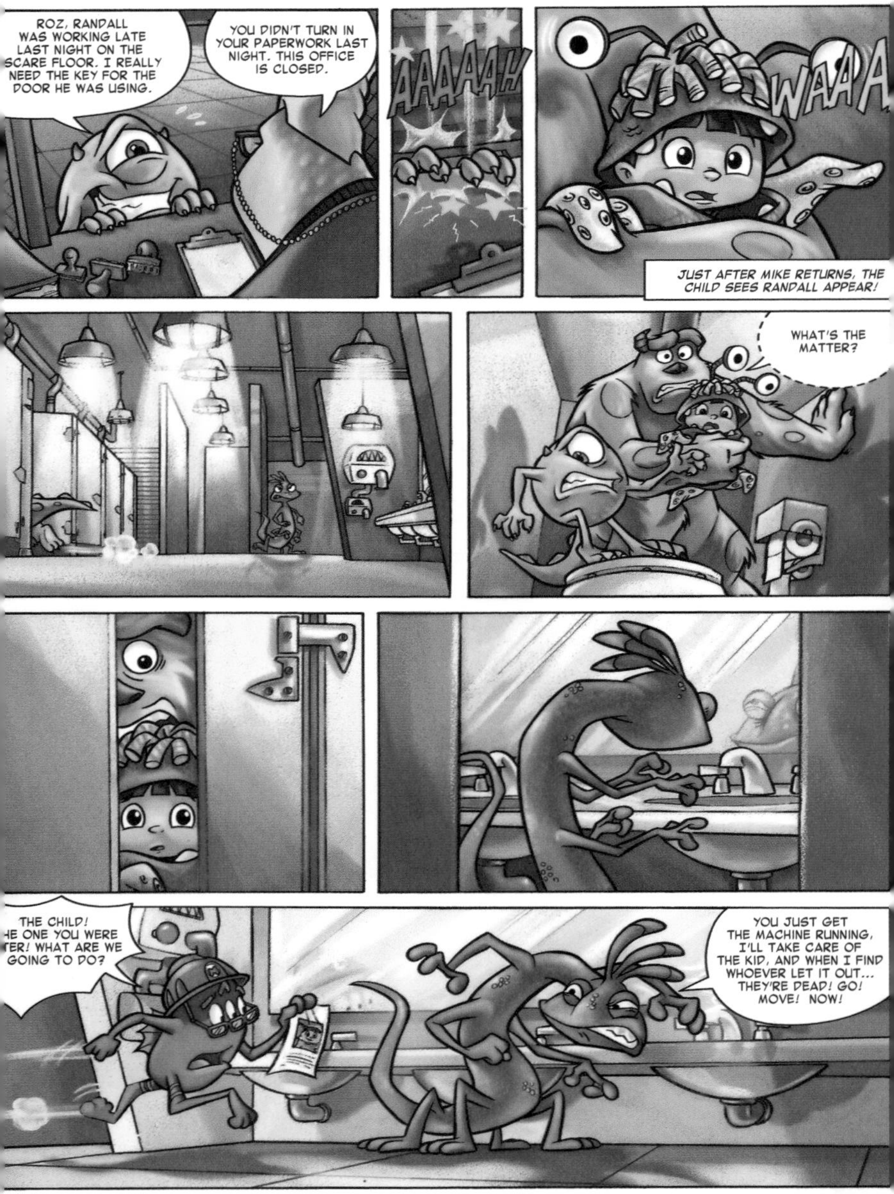

ROZ, RANDALL WAS WORKING LATE LAST NIGHT ON THE SCARE FLOOR. I REALLY NEED THE KEY FOR THE DOOR HE WAS USING.
YOU DIDN'T TURN IN YOUR PAPERWORK LAST NIGHT. THIS OFFICE IS CLOSED.
AAAAAAH
WAAA
JUST AFTER MIKE RETURNS, THE CHILD SEES RANDALL APPEAR!
WHAT'S THE MATTER?
THE CHILD! HE ONE YOU WERE TER! WHAT ARE WE GOING TO DO?
YOU JUST GET THE MACHINE RUNNING, I'LL TAKE CARE OF THE KID, AND WHEN I FIND WHOEVER LET IT OUT... THEY'RE DEAD! GO! MOVE! NOW!

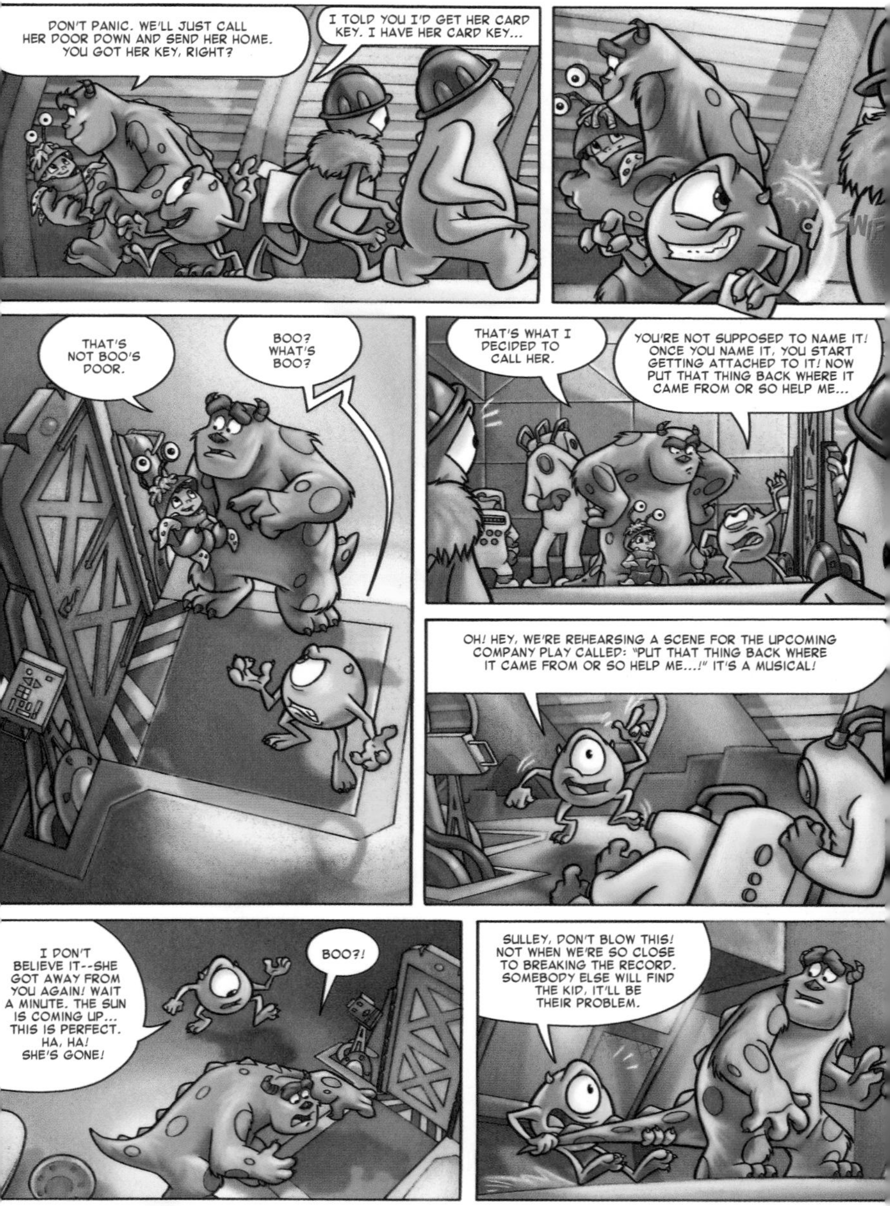
DON'T PANIC. WE'LL JUST CALL HER DOOR DOWN AND SEND HER HOME. YOU GOT HER KEY, RIGHT?
I TOLD YOU I'D GET HER CARD KEY. I HAVE HER CARD KEY...
SWIF
THAT'S NOT BOO'S DOOR.
BOO? WHAT'S BOO?
THAT'S WHAT I DECIDED TO CALL HER.
YOU'RE NOT SUPPOSED TO NAME IT! ONCE YOU NAME IT, YOU START GETTING ATTACHED TO IT! NOW PUT THAT THING BACK WHERE IT CAME FROM OR SO HELP ME...
OH! HEY, WE'RE REHEARSING A SCENE FOR THE UPCOMING COMPANY PLAY CALLED: "PUT THAT THING BACK WHERE IT CAME FROM OR SO HELP ME...!" IT'S A MUSICAL!
I DON'T BELIEVE IT--SHE GOT AWAY FROM YOU AGAIN! WAIT A MINUTE. THE SUN IS COMING UP... THIS IS PERFECT. HA, HA! SHE'S GONE!
BOO?!
SULLEY, DON'T BLOW THIS! NOT WHEN WE'RE SO CLOSE TO BREAKING THE RECORD. SOMEBODY ELSE WILL FIND THE KID, IT'LL BE THEIR PROBLEM.

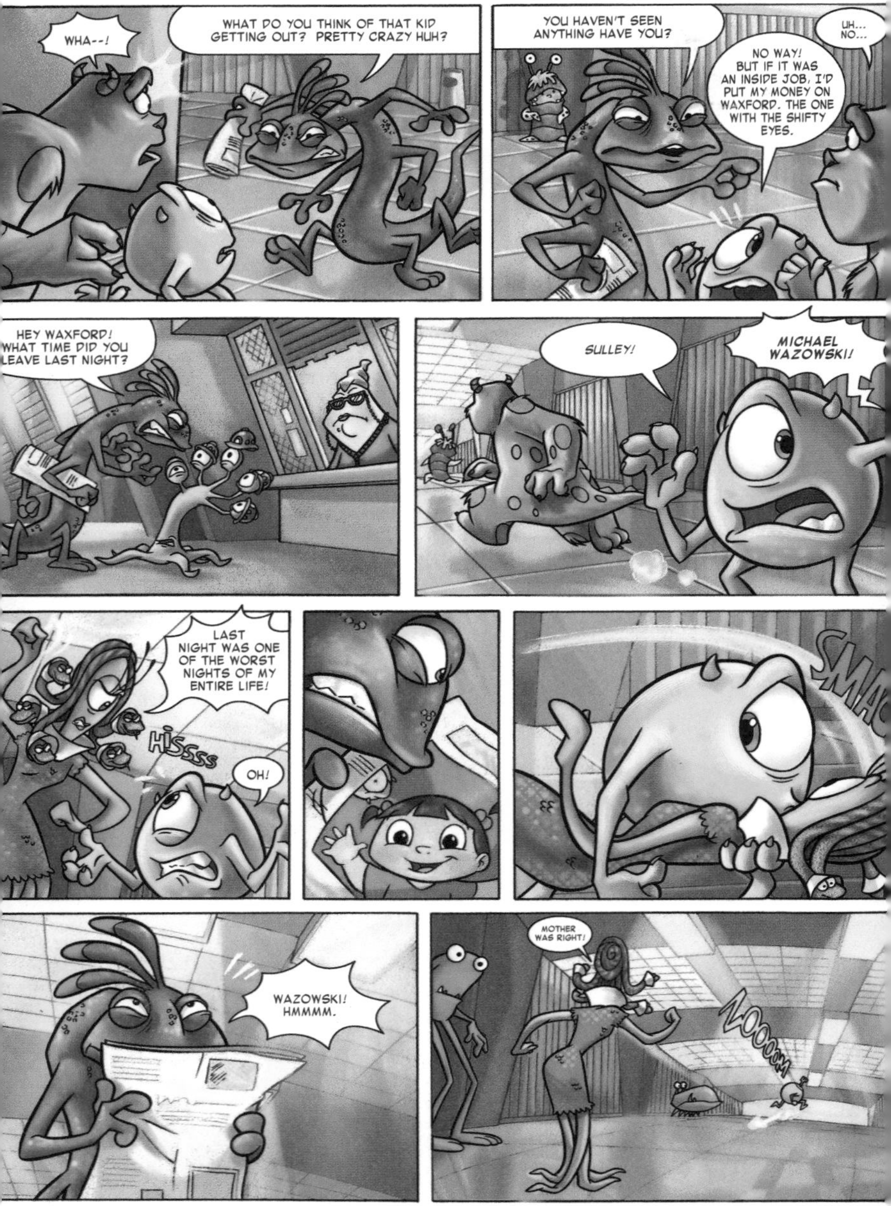
WHA--!
WHAT DO YOU THINK OF THAT KID GETTING OUT? PRETTY CRAZY HUH?
YOU HAVEN'T SEEN ANYTHING HAVE YOU?
UH... NO...
NO WAY! BUT IF IT WAS AN INSIDE JOB, I'D PUT MY MONEY ON WAXFORD. THE ONE WITH THE SHIFTY EYES.
HEY WAXFORD! WHAT TIME DID YOU LEAVE LAST NIGHT?
SULLEY!
MICHAEL WAZOWSKI!
LAST NIGHT WAS ONE OF THE WORST NIGHTS OF MY ENTIRE LIFE!
HISSSS
OH!
WAZOWSKI! HMMMM.
MOTHER WAS RIGHT!
ZOOOOM

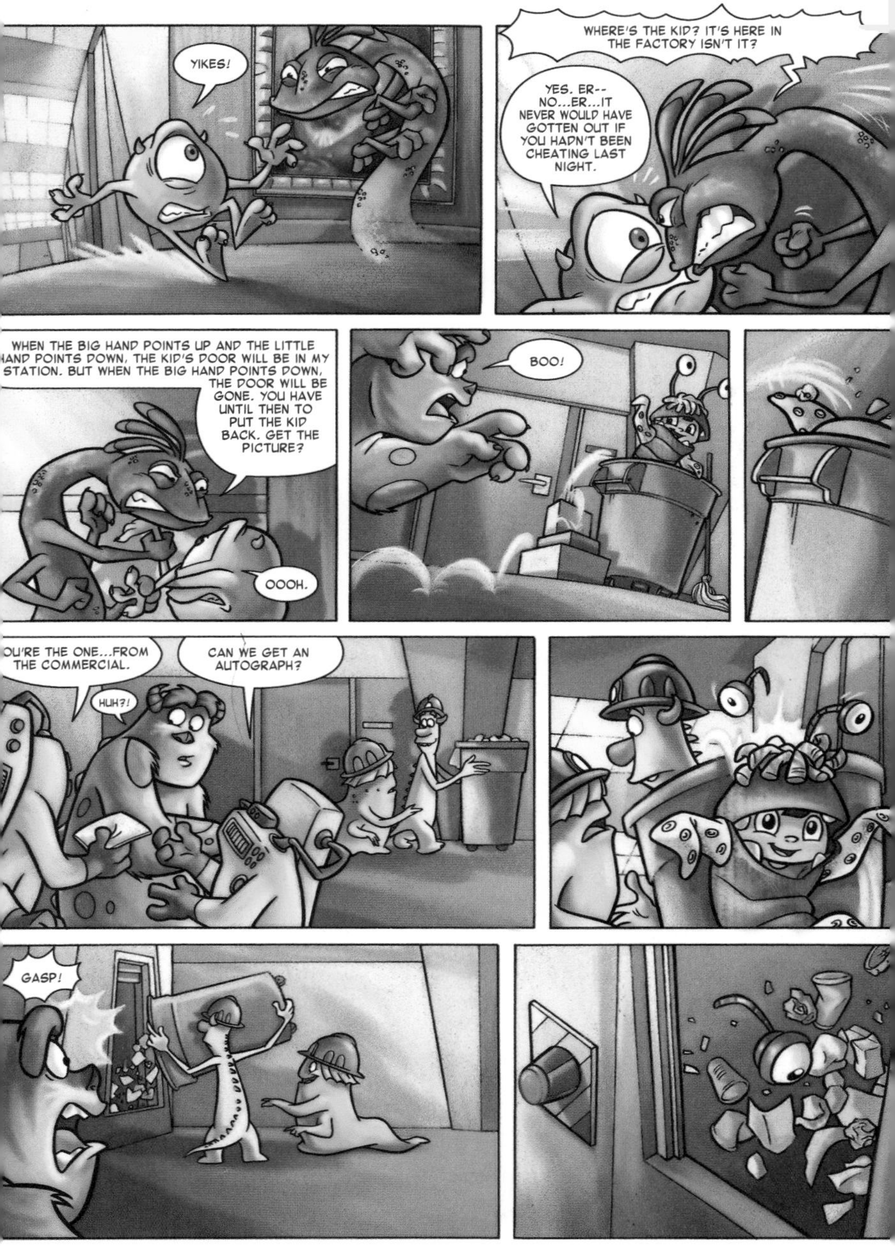
YIKES!
WHERE'S THE KID? IT'S HERE IN THE FACTORY ISN'T IT?
YES. ER-- NO...ER...IT NEVER WOULD HAVE GOTTEN OUT IF YOU HADN'T BEEN CHEATING LAST NIGHT.
WHEN THE BIG HAND POINTS UP AND THE LITTLE HAND POINTS DOWN, THE KID'S DOOR WILL BE IN MY STATION. BUT WHEN THE BIG HAND POINTS DOWN, THE DOOR WILL BE GONE. YOU HAVE UNTIL THEN TO PUT THE KID BACK. GET THE PICTURE?
OOOH.
BOO!
OU'RE THE ONE...FROM THE COMMERCIAL.
HUH?!
CAN WE GET AN AUTOGRAPH?
GASP!

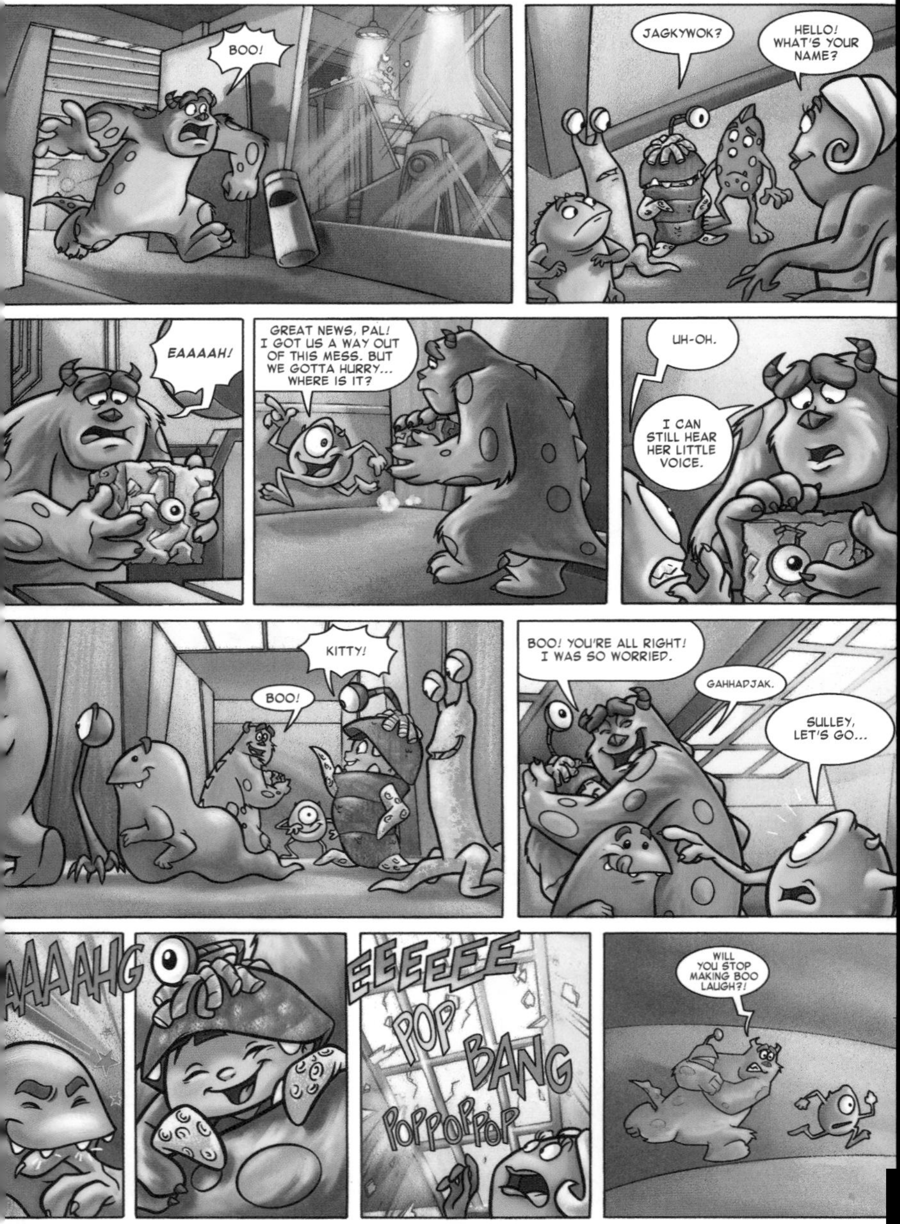
BOO!
JAGKYWOK?
HELLO! WHAT'S YOUR NAME?
EAAAAH!
GREAT NEWS, PAL! I GOT US A WAY OUT OF THIS MESS. BUT WE GOTTA HURRY... WHERE IS IT?
UH-OH.
I CAN STILL HEAR HER LITTLE VOICE.
KITTY!
BOO!
BOO! YOU'RE ALL RIGHT! I WAS SO WORRIED.
GAHHADJAK.
SULLEY, LET'S GO...
AAAAHG
EEEEEE
POP
BANG
POPPOPPOP
WILL YOU STOP MAKING BOO LAUGH?!

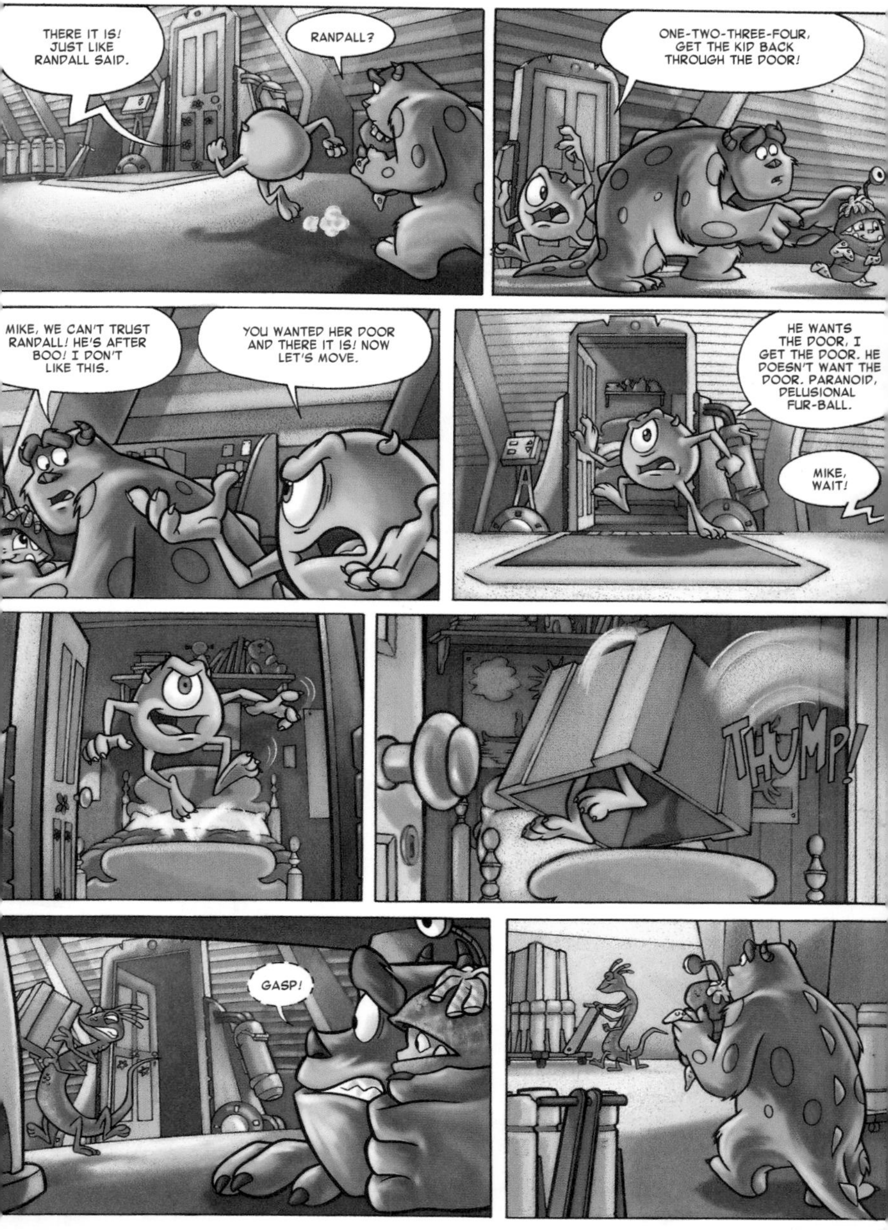
THERE IT IS! JUST LIKE RANDALL SAID.
RANDALL?
ONE-TWO-THREE-FOUR, GET THE KID BACK THROUGH THE DOOR!
MIKE, WE CAN'T TRUST RANDALL! HE'S AFTER BOO! I DON'T LIKE THIS.
YOU WANTED HER DOOR AND THERE IT IS! NOW LET'S MOVE.
HE WANTS THE DOOR, I GET THE DOOR. HE DOESN'T WANT THE DOOR. PARANOID, DELUSIONAL FUR-BALL.
MIKE, WAIT!
THUMP!
GASP!

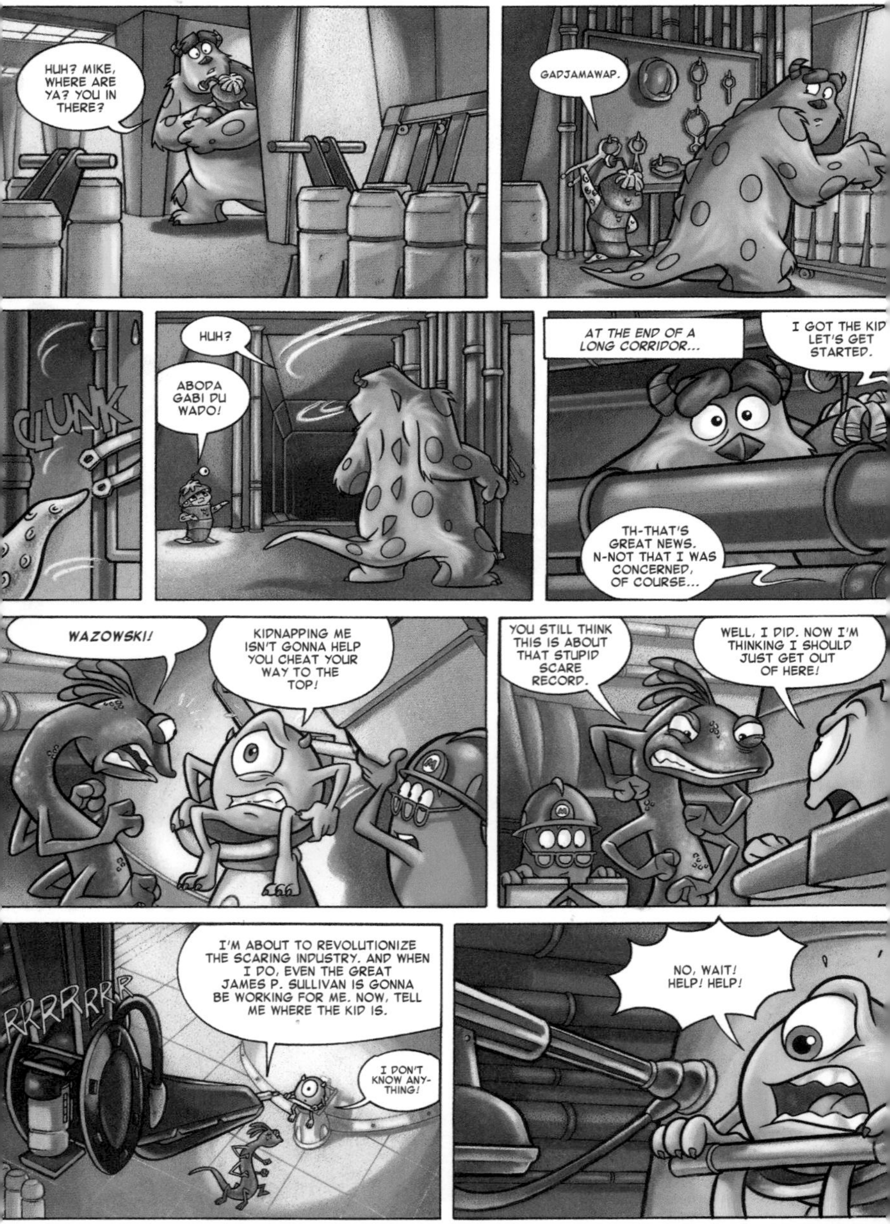
HUH? MIKE, WHERE ARE YA? YOU IN THERE?
GADJAMAWAP.
CLUNK
HUH?
ABODA GABI DU WADO!
AT THE END OF A LONG CORRIDOR...
I GOT THE KID LET'S GET STARTED.
TH-THAT'S GREAT NEWS. N-NOT THAT I WAS CONCERNED, OF COURSE...
WAZOWSKI!
KIDNAPPING ME ISN'T GONNA HELP YOU CHEAT YOUR WAY TO THE TOP!
YOU STILL THINK THIS IS ABOUT THAT STUPID SCARE RECORD.
WELL, I DID. NOW I'M THINKING I SHOULD JUST GET OUT OF HERE!
I'M ABOUT TO REVOLUTIONIZE THE SCARING INDUSTRY. AND WHEN I DO, EVEN THE GREAT JAMES P. SULLIVAN IS GONNA BE WORKING FOR ME. NOW, TELL ME WHERE THE KID IS.
RRRRRRRR
I DON'T KNOW ANY-THING!
NO, WAIT! HELP! HELP!

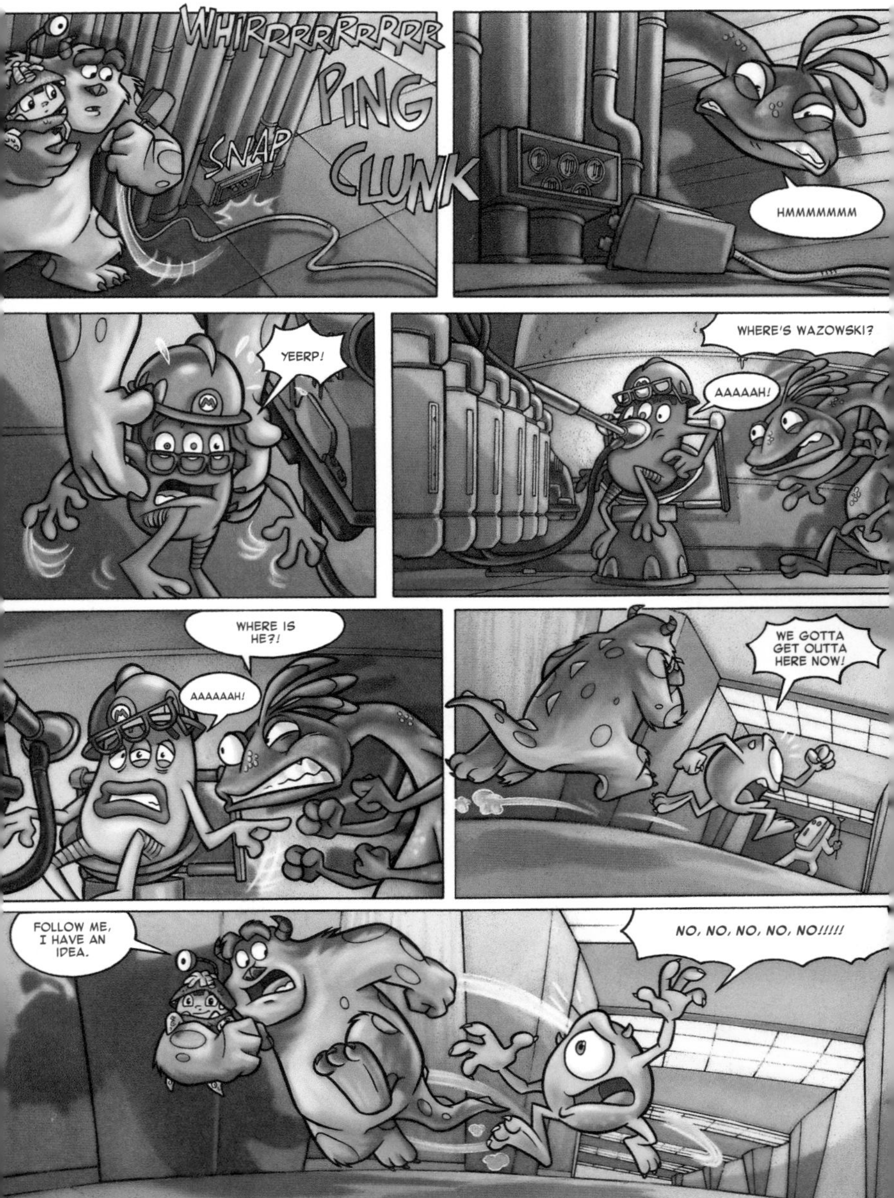
WHIRRRRRRRRR
PING
SNAP
CLUNK
HMMMMMMM
YEERP!
WHERE'S WAZOWSKI?
AAAAAH!
WHERE IS HE?!
AAAAAAH!
WE GOTTA GET OUTTA HERE NOW!
FOLLOW ME, I HAVE AN IDEA.
NO, NO, NO, NO, NO!!!!!

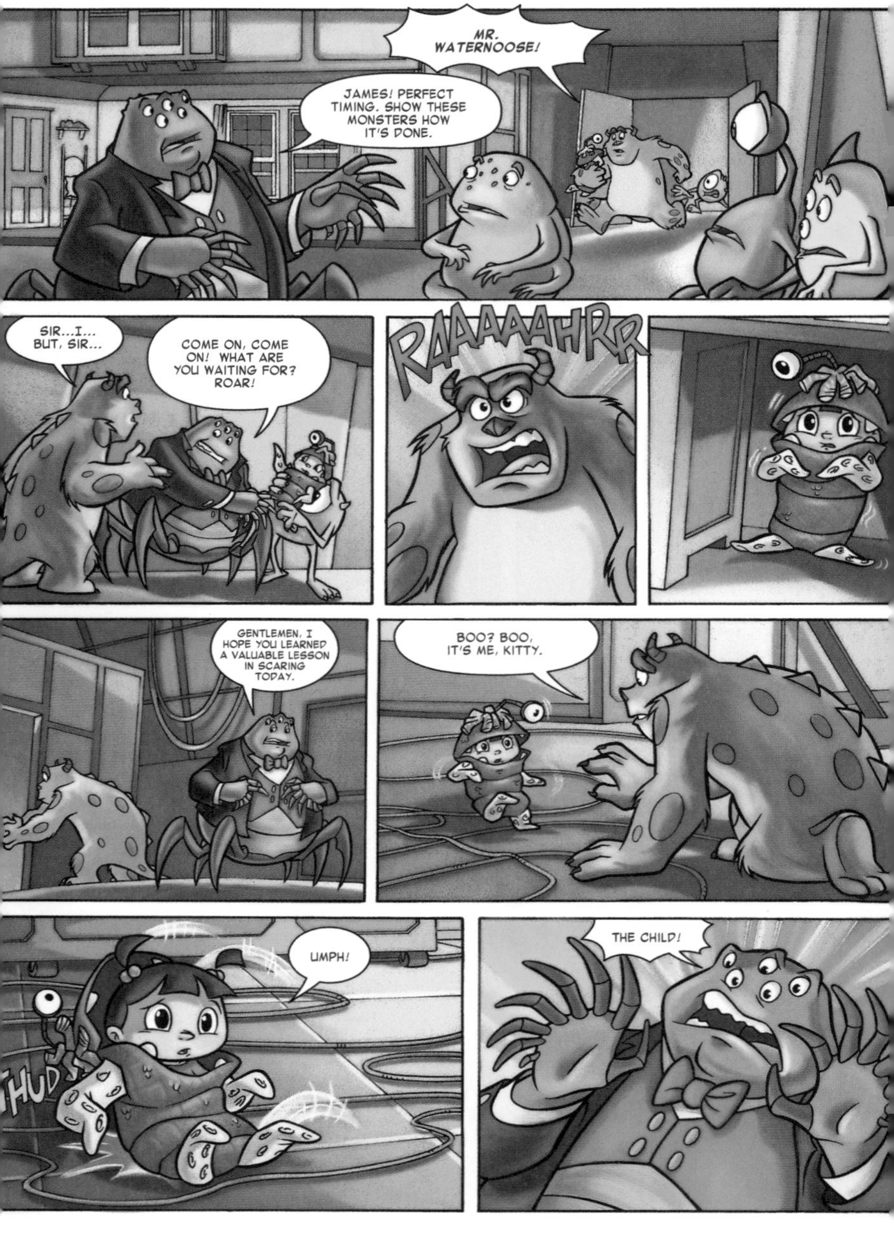
MR. WATERNOOSE!
JAMES! PERFECT TIMING. SHOW THESE MONSTERS HOW IT'S DONE.
SIR...I... BUT, SIR...
COME ON, COME ON! WHAT ARE YOU WAITING FOR? ROAR!
RAAAAAHRR
GENTLEMEN, I HOPE YOU LEARNED A VALUABLE LESSON IN SCARING TODAY.
BOO? BOO, IT'S ME, KITTY.
THUD
UMPH!
THE CHILD!

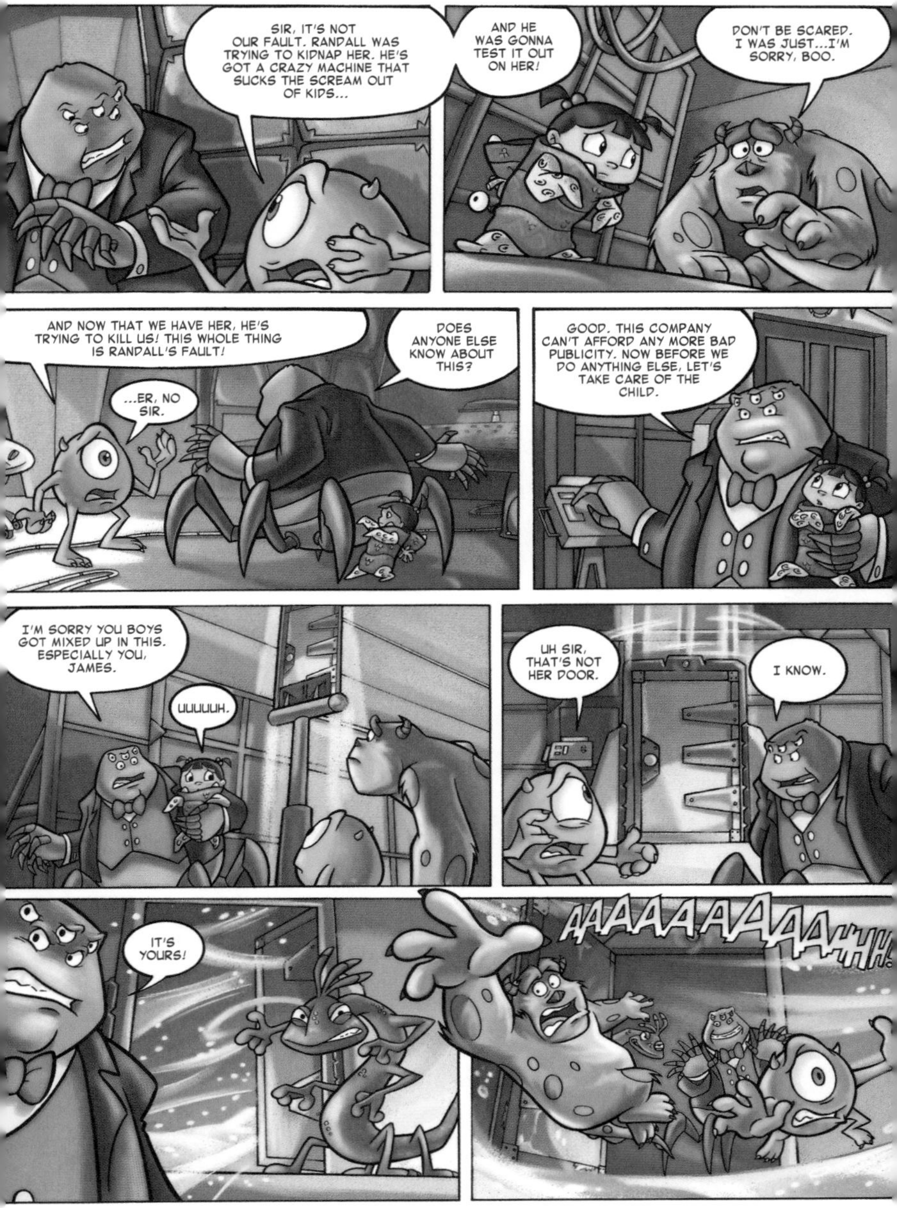
SIR, IT'S NOT OUR FAULT. RANDALL WAS TRYING TO KIDNAP HER. HE'S GOT A CRAZY MACHINE THAT SUCKS THE SCREAM OUT OF KIDS...
AND HE WAS GONNA TEST IT OUT ON HER!
DON'T BE SCARED. I WAS JUST...I'M SORRY, BOO.
AND NOW THAT WE HAVE HER, HE'S TRYING TO KILL US! THIS WHOLE THING IS RANDALL'S FAULT!
DOES ANYONE ELSE KNOW ABOUT THIS?
...ER, NO SIR.
GOOD. THIS COMPANY CAN'T AFFORD ANY MORE BAD PUBLICITY. NOW BEFORE WE DO ANYTHING ELSE, LET'S TAKE CARE OF THE CHILD.
I'M SORRY YOU BOYS GOT MIXED UP IN THIS. ESPECIALLY YOU, JAMES.
UUUUUH.
UH SIR, THAT'S NOT HER DOOR.
I KNOW.
IT'S YOURS!
AAAAAAAAAAHHH!

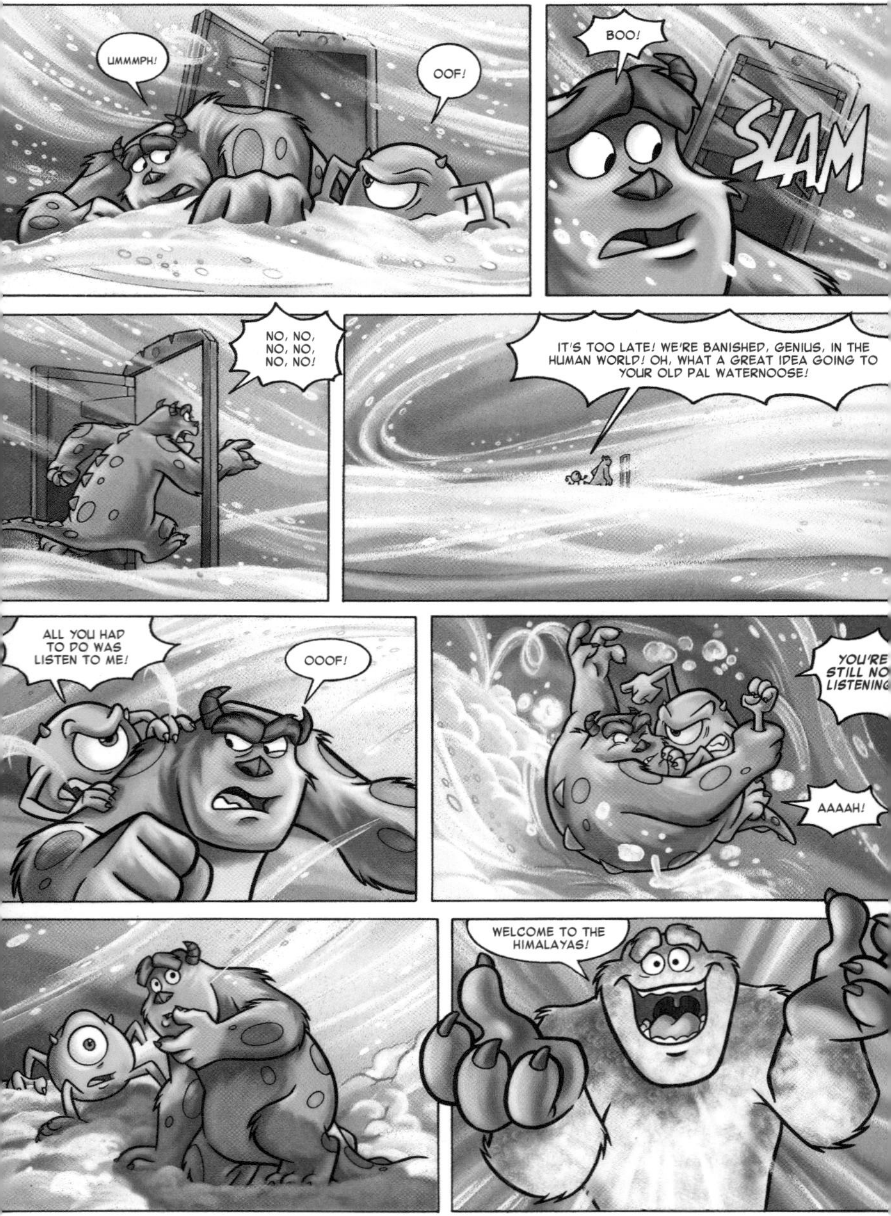
UMMMPH!
OOF!
BOO!
SLAM
NO, NO, NO, NO, NO, NO!
IT'S TOO LATE! WE'RE BANISHED, GENIUS, IN THE HUMAN WORLD! OH, WHAT A GREAT IDEA GOING TO YOUR OLD PAL WATERNOOSE!
ALL YOU HAD TO DO WAS LISTEN TO ME!
OOOF!
YOU'RE STILL NO LISTENING
AAAAH!
WELCOME TO THE HIMALAYAS!

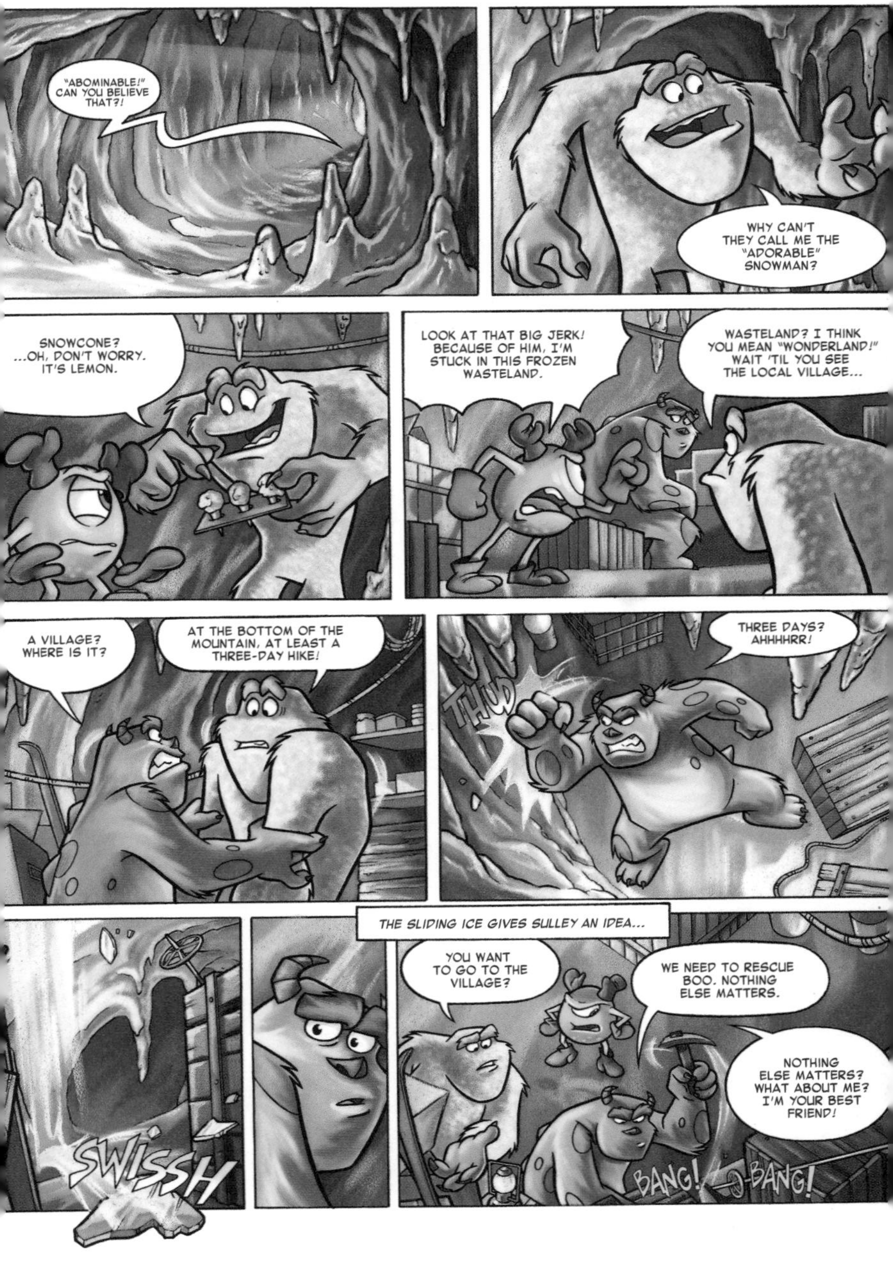
"ABOMINABLE!" CAN YOU BELIEVE THAT?!
WHY CAN'T THEY CALL ME THE "ADORABLE" SNOWMAN?
SNOWCONE? ...OH, DON'T WORRY. IT'S LEMON.
LOOK AT THAT BIG JERK! BECAUSE OF HIM, I'M STUCK IN THIS FROZEN WASTELAND.
WASTELAND? I THINK YOU MEAN "WONDERLAND!" WAIT 'TIL YOU SEE THE LOCAL VILLAGE...
A VILLAGE? WHERE IS IT?
AT THE BOTTOM OF THE MOUNTAIN, AT LEAST A THREE-DAY HIKE!
THREE DAYS? AHHHHRR!
THUD
THE SLIDING ICE GIVES SULLEY AN IDEA...
SWISSH
YOU WANT TO GO TO THE VILLAGE?
WE NEED TO RESCUE BOO. NOTHING ELSE MATTERS.
NOTHING ELSE MATTERS? WHAT ABOUT ME? I'M YOUR BEST FRIEND!
BANG!
BANG!

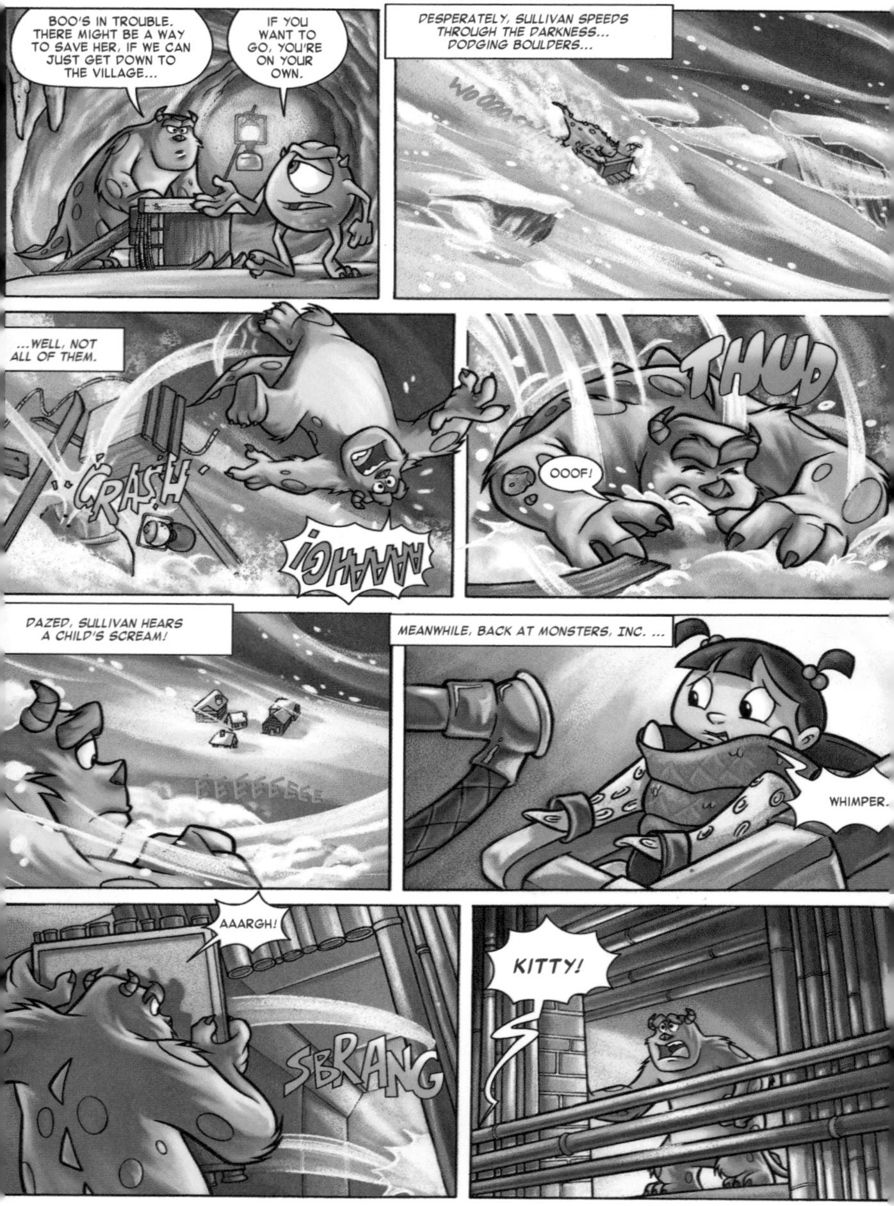
BOO'S IN TROUBLE. THERE MIGHT BE A WAY TO SAVE HER, IF WE CAN JUST GET DOWN TO THE VILLAGE...
IF YOU WANT TO GO, YOU'RE ON YOUR OWN.
DESPERATELY, SULLIVAN SPEEDS THROUGH THE DARKNESS... DODGING BOULDERS...
...WELL, NOT ALL OF THEM.
CRASH
THUD
OOOF!
DAZED, SULLIVAN HEARS A CHILD'S SCREAM!
MEANWHILE, BACK AT MONSTERS, INC. ...
WHIMPER.
AAARGH!
SBRANG
KITTY!

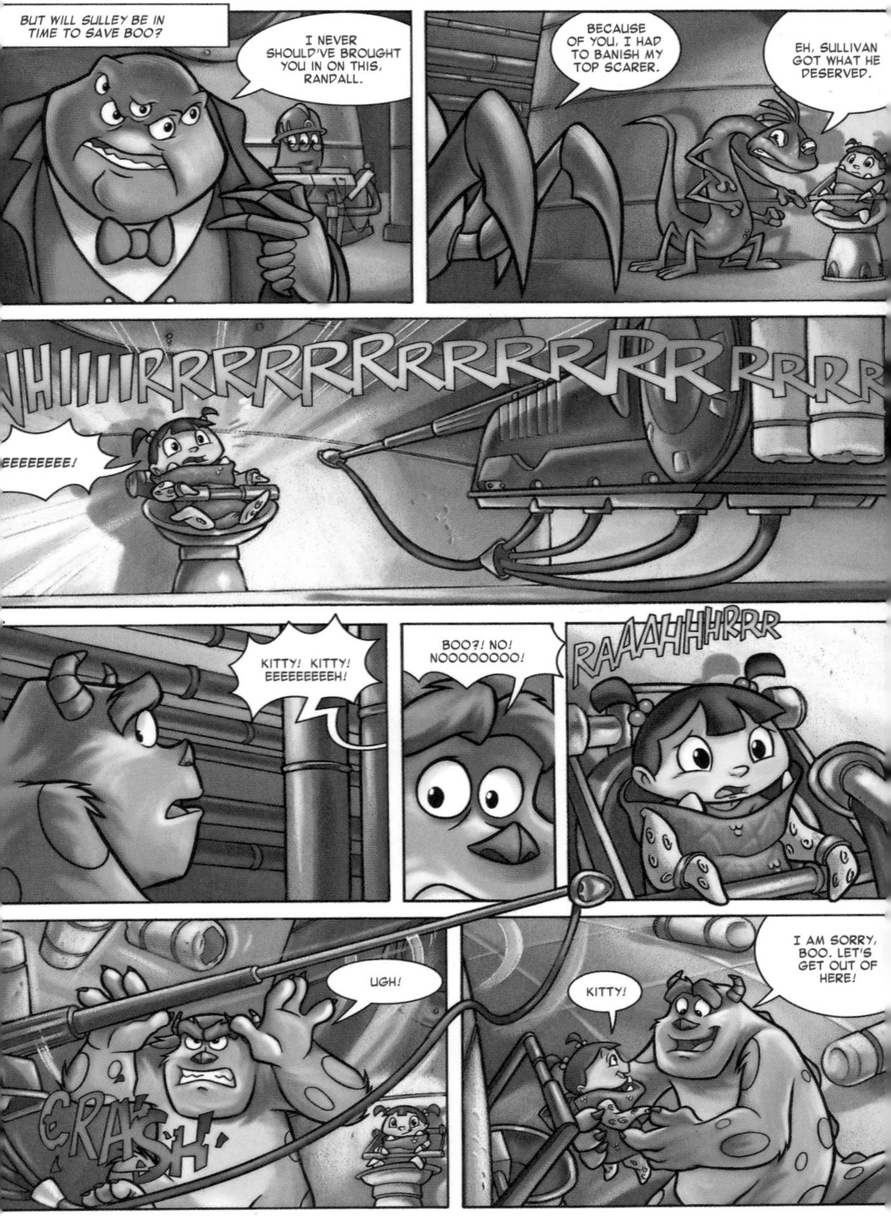
BUT WILL SULLEY BE IN TIME TO SAVE BOO?
I NEVER SHOULD'VE BROUGHT YOU IN ON THIS, RANDALL.
BECAUSE OF YOU, I HAD TO BANISH MY TOP SCARER.
EH, SULLIVAN GOT WHAT HE DESERVED.
JHIIIIRRRRRRRRRRRRRRR
EEEEEEEE!
KITTY! KITTY! EEEEEEEEEH!
BOO?! NO! NOOOOOOOO!
RAAAHHHRRR
UGH!
CRASH!
KITTY!
I AM SORRY, BOO. LET'S GET OUT OF HERE!

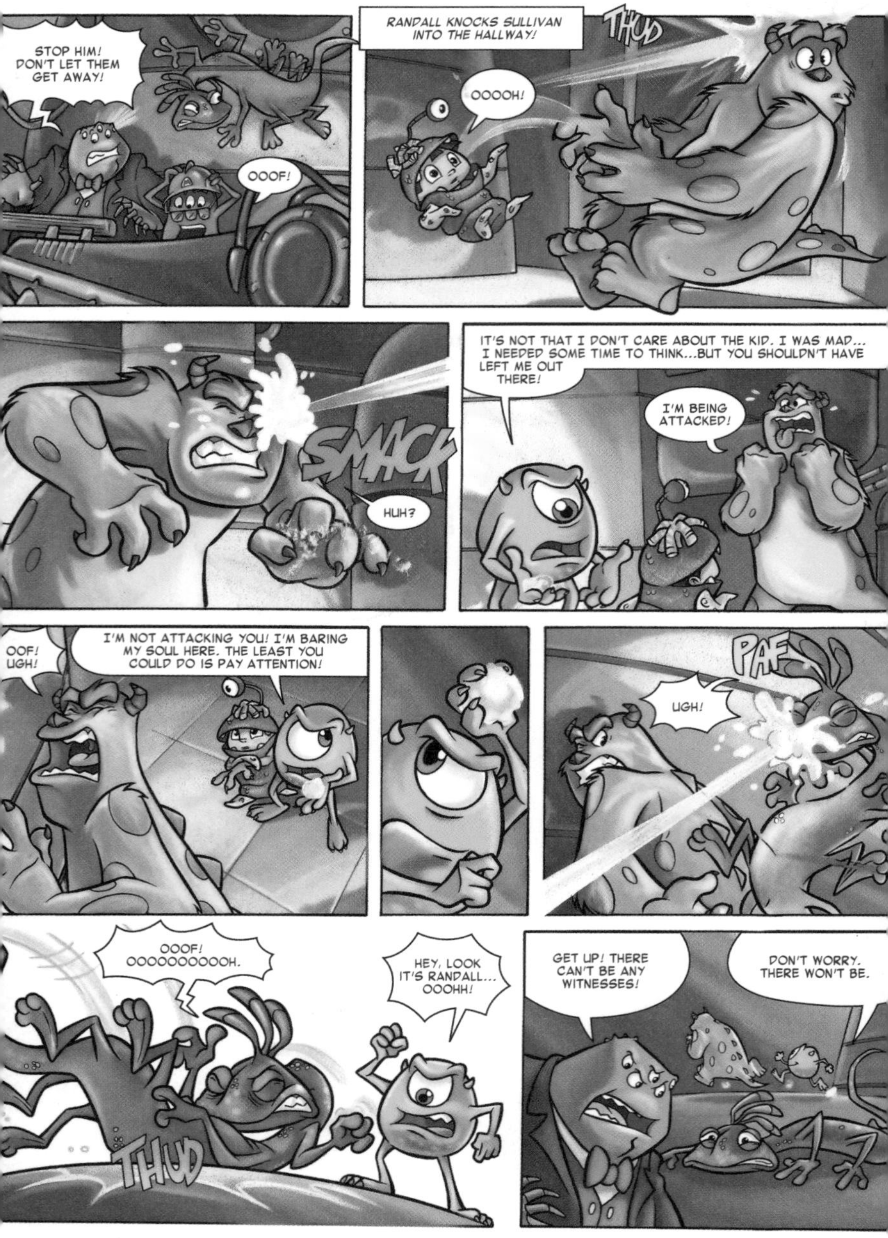
STOP HIM! DON'T LET THEM GET AWAY!
OOOF!
RANDALL KNOCKS SULLIVAN INTO THE HALLWAY!
THUD
OOOOH!
SMACK
HUH?
IT'S NOT THAT I DON'T CARE ABOUT THE KID. I WAS MAD... I NEEDED SOME TIME TO THINK...BUT YOU SHOULDN'T HAVE LEFT ME OUT THERE!
I'M BEING ATTACKED!
OOF! UGH!
I'M NOT ATTACKING YOU! I'M BARING MY SOUL HERE. THE LEAST YOU COULD DO IS PAY ATTENTION!
PAF
UGH!
OOOF! OOOOOOOOOOH.
THUD
HEY, LOOK IT'S RANDALL... OOOHH!
GET UP! THERE CAN'T BE ANY WITNESSES!
DON'T WORRY. THERE WON'T BE.

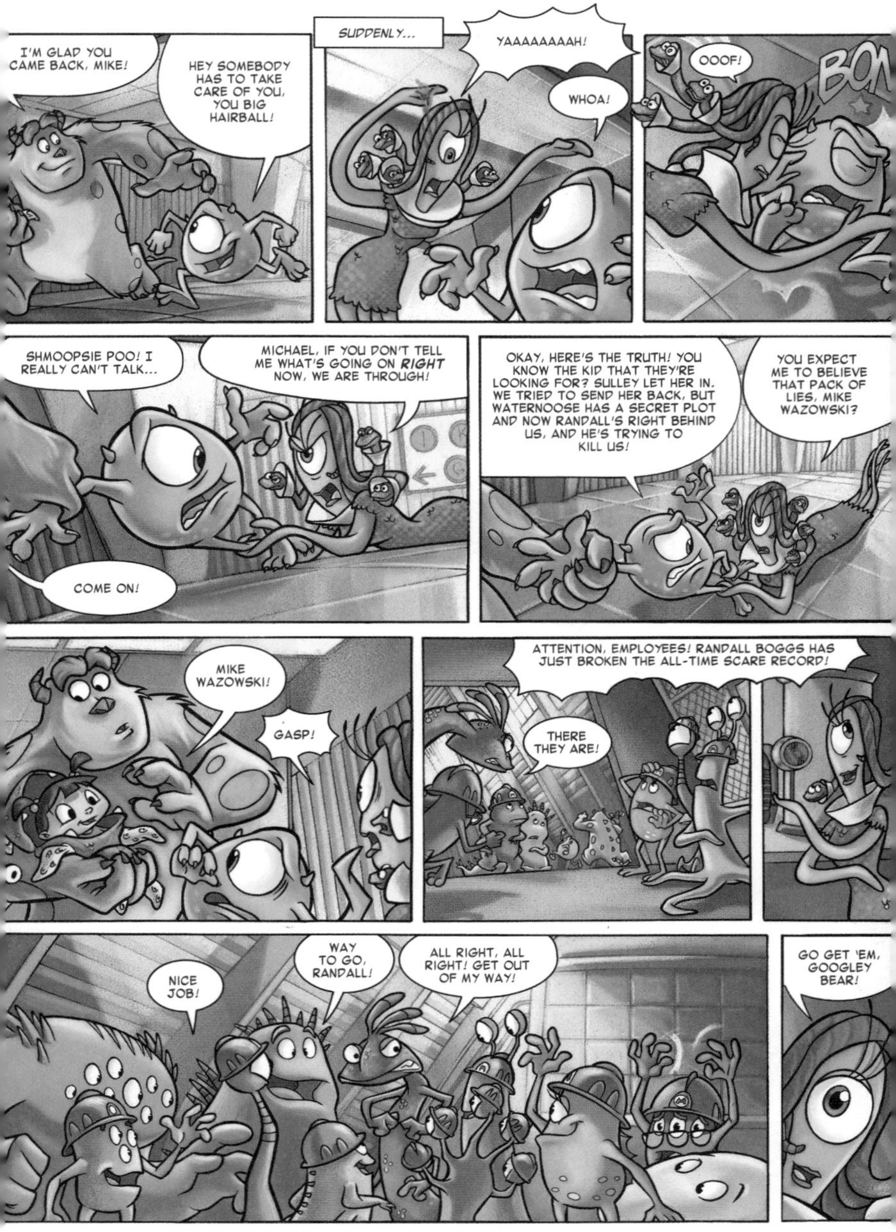
I'M GLAD YOU CAME BACK, MIKE!
HEY SOMEBODY HAS TO TAKE CARE OF YOU, YOU BIG HAIRBALL!
SUDDENLY...
YAAAAAAAAH!
WHOA!
OOOF!
BOM
SHMOOPSIE POO! I REALLY CAN'T TALK...
MICHAEL, IF YOU DON'T TELL ME WHAT'S GOING ON RIGHT NOW, WE ARE THROUGH!
COME ON!
OKAY, HERE'S THE TRUTH! YOU KNOW THE KID THAT THEY'RE LOOKING FOR? SULLEY LET HER IN. WE TRIED TO SEND HER BACK, BUT WATERNOOSE HAS A SECRET PLOT AND NOW RANDALL'S RIGHT BEHIND US, AND HE'S TRYING TO KILL US!
YOU EXPECT ME TO BELIEVE THAT PACK OF LIES, MIKE WAZOWSKI?
MIKE WAZOWSKI!
GASP!
ATTENTION, EMPLOYEES! RANDALL BOGGS HAS JUST BROKEN THE ALL-TIME SCARE RECORD!
THERE THEY ARE!
NICE JOB!
WAY TO GO, RANDALL!
ALL RIGHT, ALL RIGHT! GET OUT OF MY WAY!
GO GET 'EM, GOOGLEY BEAR!

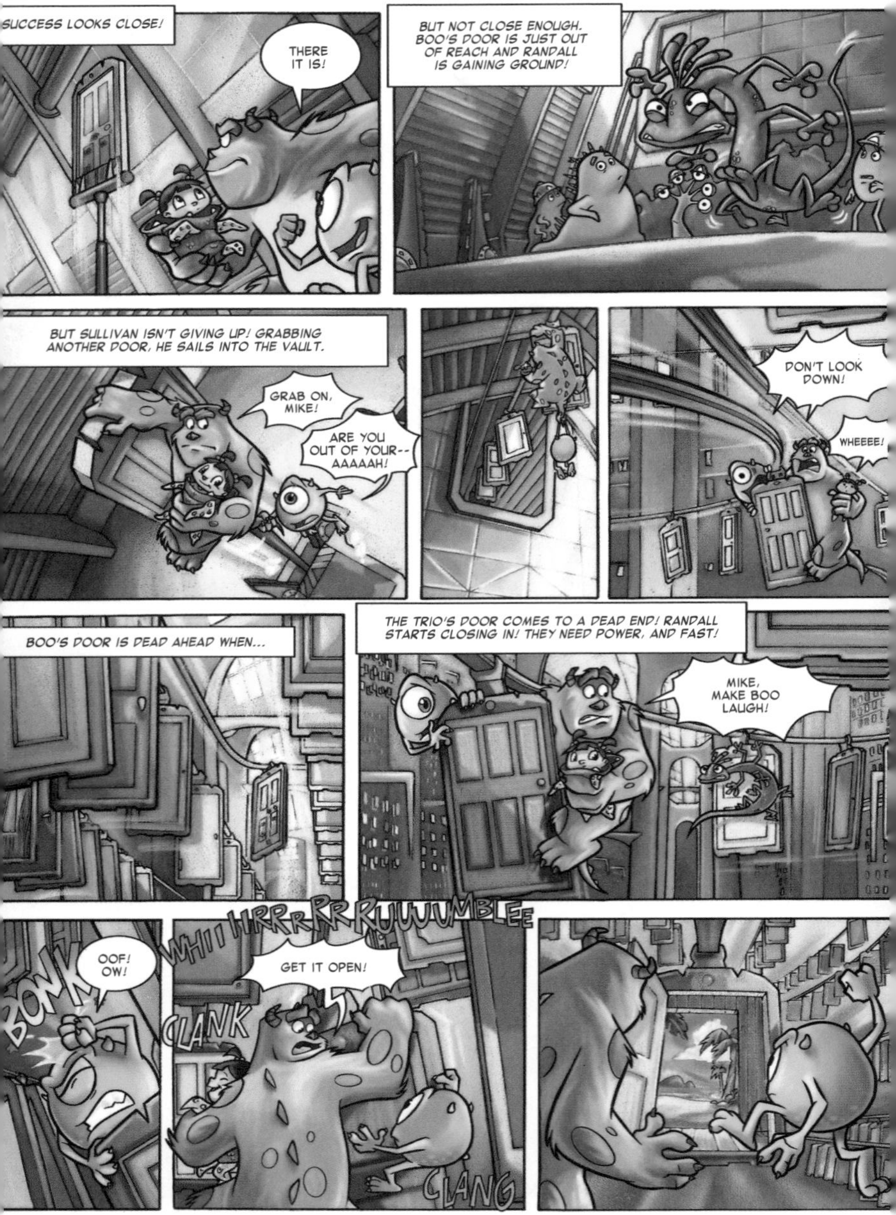
SUCCESS LOOKS CLOSE!
THERE IT IS!
BUT NOT CLOSE ENOUGH. BOO'S DOOR IS JUST OUT OF REACH AND RANDALL IS GAINING GROUND!
BUT SULLIVAN ISN'T GIVING UP! GRABBING ANOTHER DOOR, HE SAILS INTO THE VAULT.
GRAB ON, MIKE!
ARE YOU OUT OF YOUR-- AAAAAH!
DON'T LOOK DOWN!
WHEEEE!
BOO'S DOOR IS DEAD AHEAD WHEN...
THE TRIO'S DOOR COMES TO A DEAD END! RANDALL STARTS CLOSING IN! THEY NEED POWER, AND FAST!
MIKE, MAKE BOO LAUGH!
BONK
OOF! OW!
WHIIIIRRRRRRRUUUUMBLEE
GET IT OPEN!
CLANK
CLANG

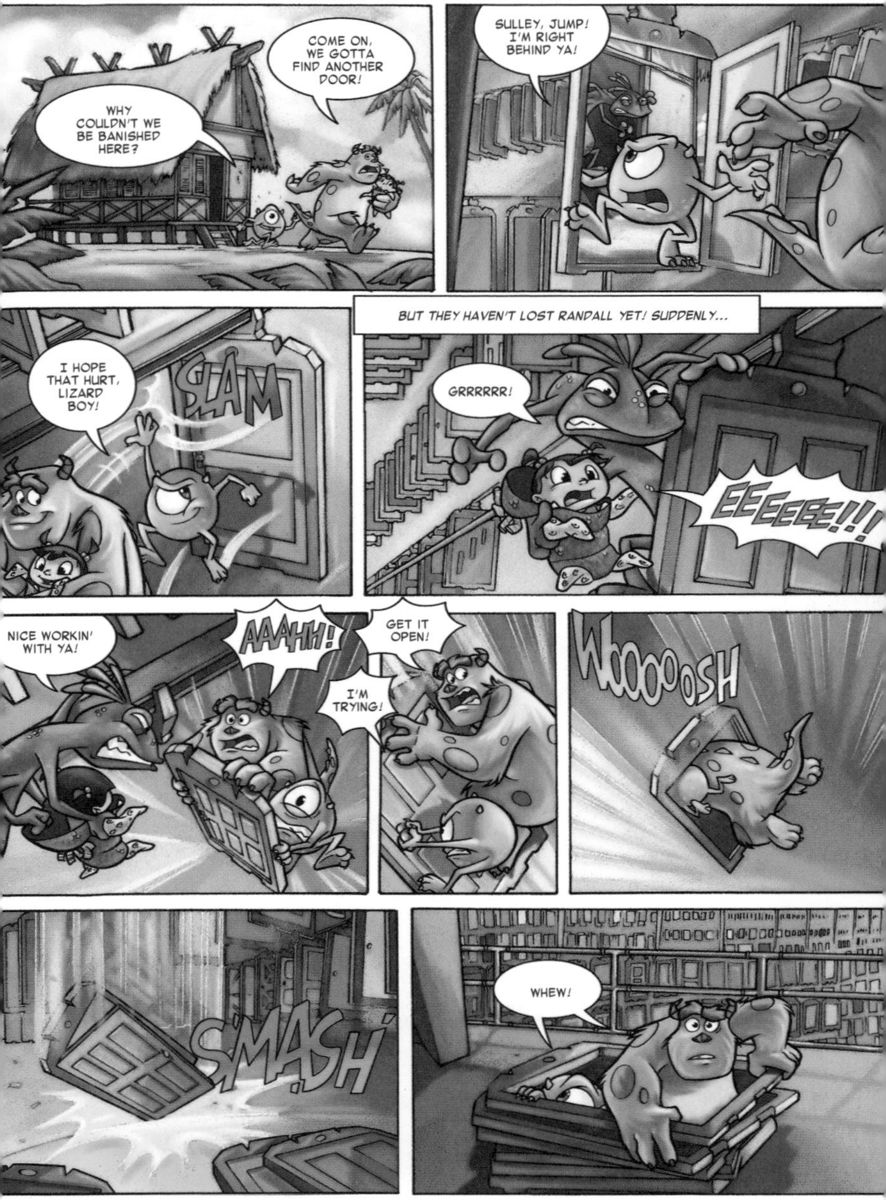
WHY COULDN'T WE BE BANISHED HERE?
COME ON, WE GOTTA FIND ANOTHER DOOR!
SULLEY, JUMP! I'M RIGHT BEHIND YA!
I HOPE THAT HURT, LIZARD BOY!
SLAM
BUT THEY HAVEN'T LOST RANDALL YET! SUDDENLY...
GRRRRRR!
EEEEEE!!!
NICE WORKIN' WITH YA!
AAAHH!
GET IT OPEN!
I'M TRYING!
WOOOOOSH
SMASH
WHEW!

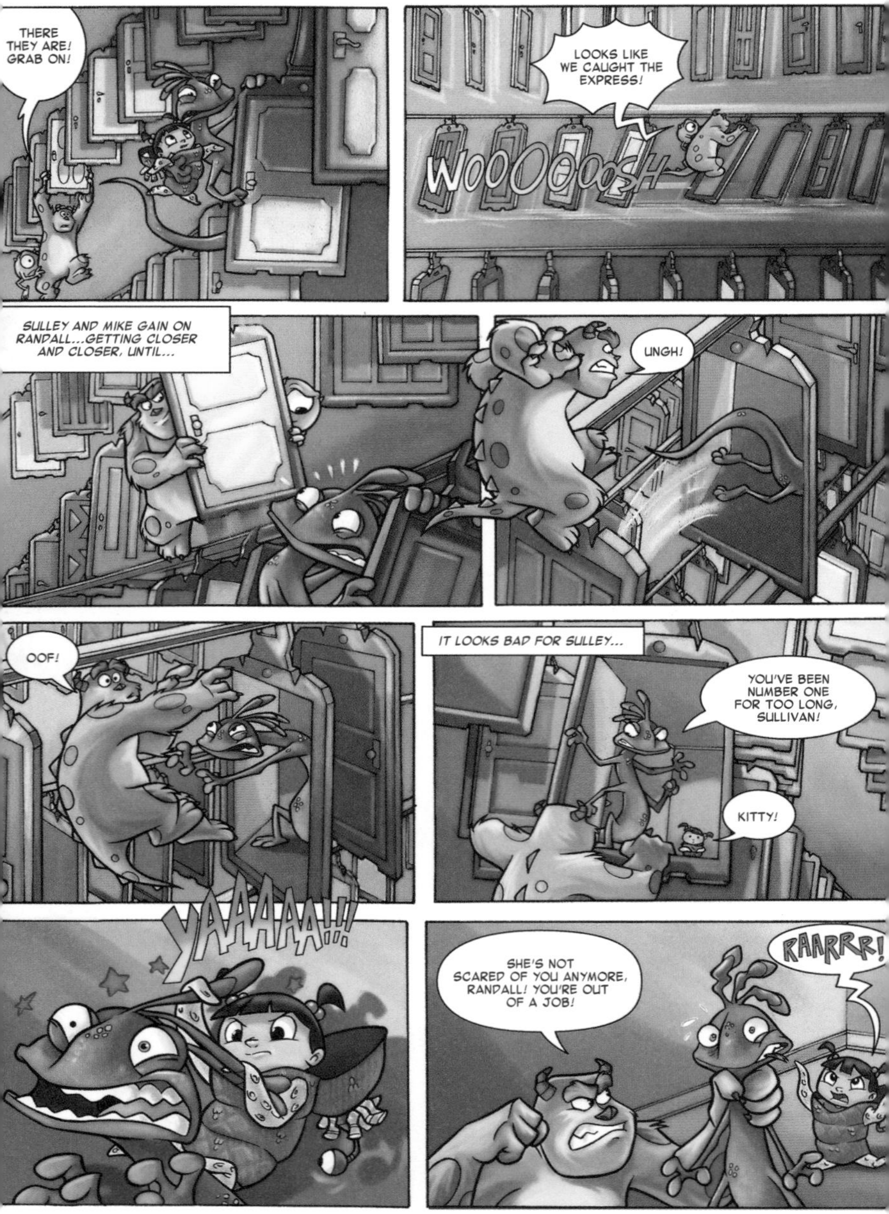
THERE THEY ARE! GRAB ON!
LOOKS LIKE WE CAUGHT THE EXPRESS!
WOOOOOOSH
SULLEY AND MIKE GAIN ON RANDALL...GETTING CLOSER AND CLOSER, UNTIL...
UNGH!
OOF!
IT LOOKS BAD FOR SULLEY...
YOU'VE BEEN NUMBER ONE FOR TOO LONG, SULLIVAN!
KITTY!
YAAAAA!!!
SHE'S NOT SCARED OF YOU ANYMORE, RANDALL! YOU'RE OUT OF A JOB!
RAARRR!

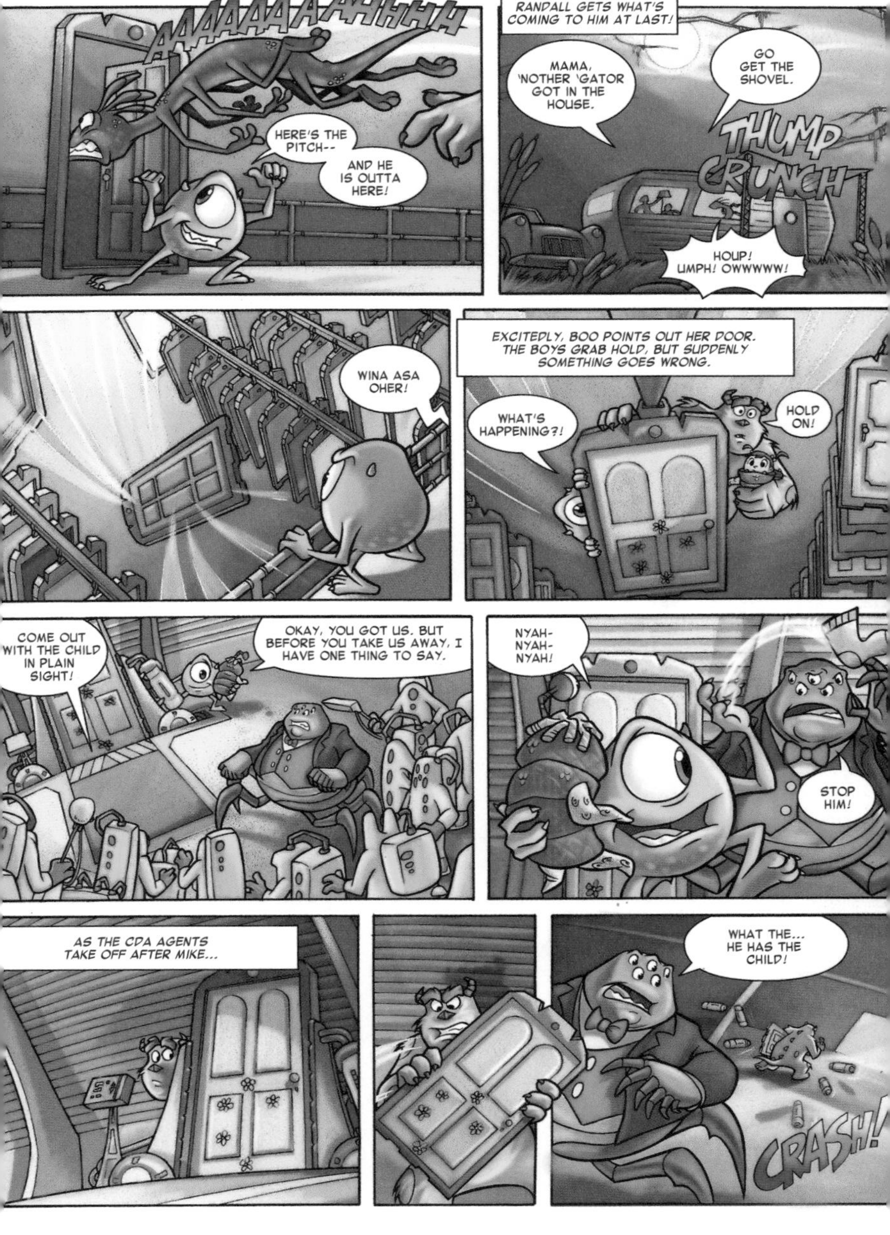
AAAAAAAAHHHH
HERE'S THE PITCH--
AND HE IS OUTTA HERE!
RANDALL GETS WHAT'S COMING TO HIM AT LAST!
MAMA, 'NOTHER 'GATOR GOT IN THE HOUSE.
GO GET THE SHOVEL.
THUMP
CRUNCH
HOUP! UMPH! OWWWWW!
WINA ASA OHER!
EXCITEDLY, BOO POINTS OUT HER DOOR. THE BOYS GRAB HOLD, BUT SUDDENLY SOMETHING GOES WRONG.
WHAT'S HAPPENING?!
HOLD ON!
COME OUT WITH THE CHILD IN PLAIN SIGHT!
OKAY, YOU GOT US. BUT BEFORE YOU TAKE US AWAY, I HAVE ONE THING TO SAY.
NYAH-NYAH-NYAH!
STOP HIM!
AS THE CDA AGENTS TAKE OFF AFTER MIKE...
WHAT THE... HE HAS THE CHILD!
CRASH!

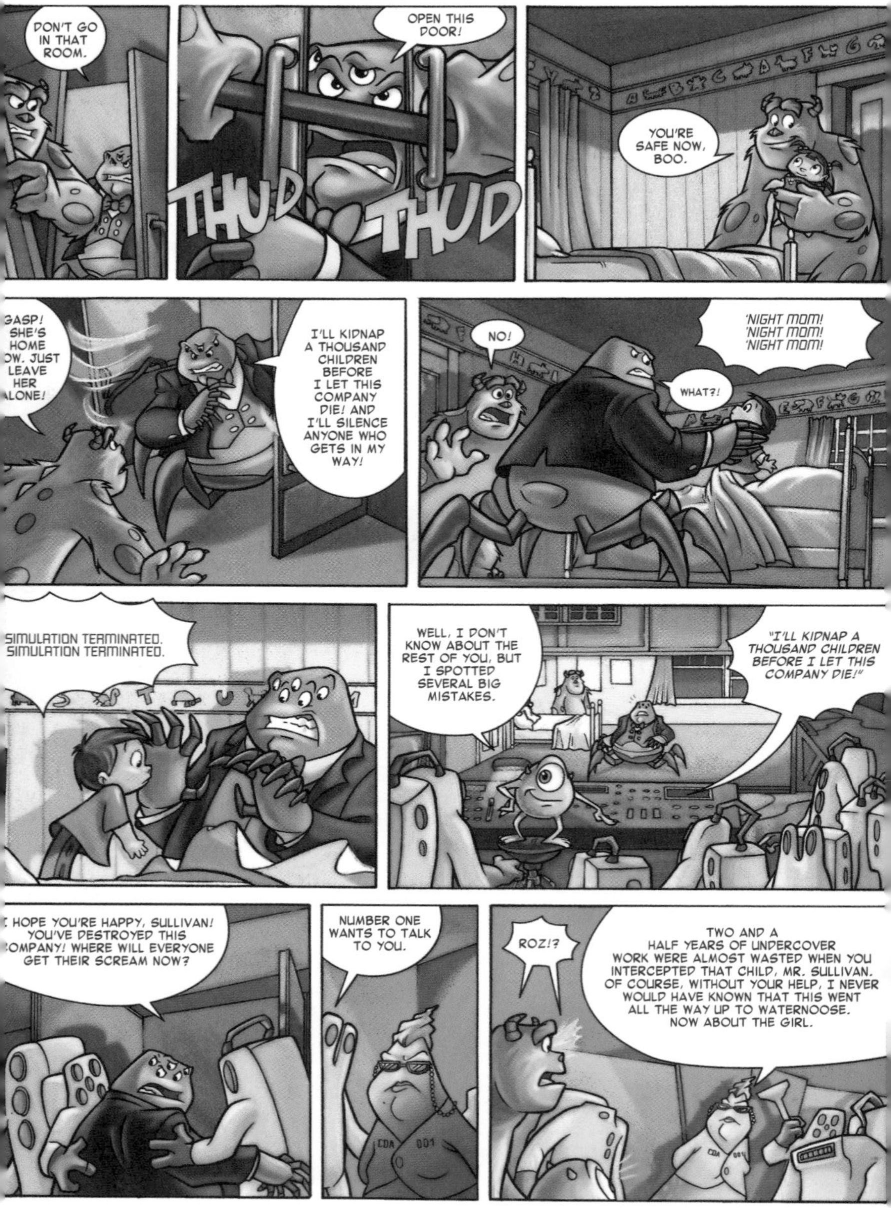
DON'T GO IN THAT ROOM.
OPEN THIS DOOR!
THUD THUD
YOU'RE SAFE NOW, BOO.
GASP! SHE'S HOME OW. JUST LEAVE HER LONE!
I'LL KIDNAP A THOUSAND CHILDREN BEFORE I LET THIS COMPANY DIE! AND I'LL SILENCE ANYONE WHO GETS IN MY WAY!
NO!
'NIGHT MOM! 'NIGHT MOM! 'NIGHT MOM!
WHAT?!
SIMULATION TERMINATED. SIMULATION TERMINATED.
WELL, I DON'T KNOW ABOUT THE REST OF YOU, BUT I SPOTTED SEVERAL BIG MISTAKES.
"I'LL KIDNAP A THOUSAND CHILDREN BEFORE I LET THIS COMPANY DIE!"
HOPE YOU'RE HAPPY, SULLIVAN! YOU'VE DESTROYED THIS OMPANY! WHERE WILL EVERYONE GET THEIR SCREAM NOW?
NUMBER ONE WANTS TO TALK TO YOU.
ROZ!?
TWO AND A HALF YEARS OF UNDERCOVER WORK WERE ALMOST WASTED WHEN YOU INTERCEPTED THAT CHILD, MR. SULLIVAN. OF COURSE, WITHOUT YOUR HELP, I NEVER WOULD HAVE KNOWN THAT THIS WENT ALL THE WAY UP TO WATERNOOSE. NOW ABOUT THE GIRL.

I JUST WANT TO SEND HER HOME.

YOU MEAN, I CAN'T SEE HER AGAIN?

VERY GOOD. SOMEONE BRING ME A DOOR SHREDDER.

THAT'S THE WAY IT HAS TO BE. I'LL GIVE YOU FIVE MINUTES.

NOTHING'S COMING OUT OF THE CLOSET TO SCARE YOU ANYMORE. RIGHT?

BABJAWADA

KITTY.

GOODBYE, BOO. KITTY HAS TO LEAVE.

TLACK

BOO! ...KITTY?

NONE OF THIS EVER HAPPENED, GENTLEMEN. AND I DON'T WANT TO SEE ANY PAPERWORK ON THIS.

RRRRRRRRRRRRRRR

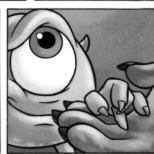

THEY'RE TAKING MR. WATERNOOSE AWAY. THE FACTORY WILL SHUT DOWN!

THERE'LL BE EVEN LESS SCREAM TO GO AROUND! EEEEEE!

CHEER UP, PAL. WE GOT HER HOME. ALL RIGHT, WE'RE BOTH OUT OF A JOB; BUT YOU KNOW, WE HAD SOME LAUGHS ALONG THE WAY.

SUDDENLY, SULLIVAN HAS A BRILLIANT IDE

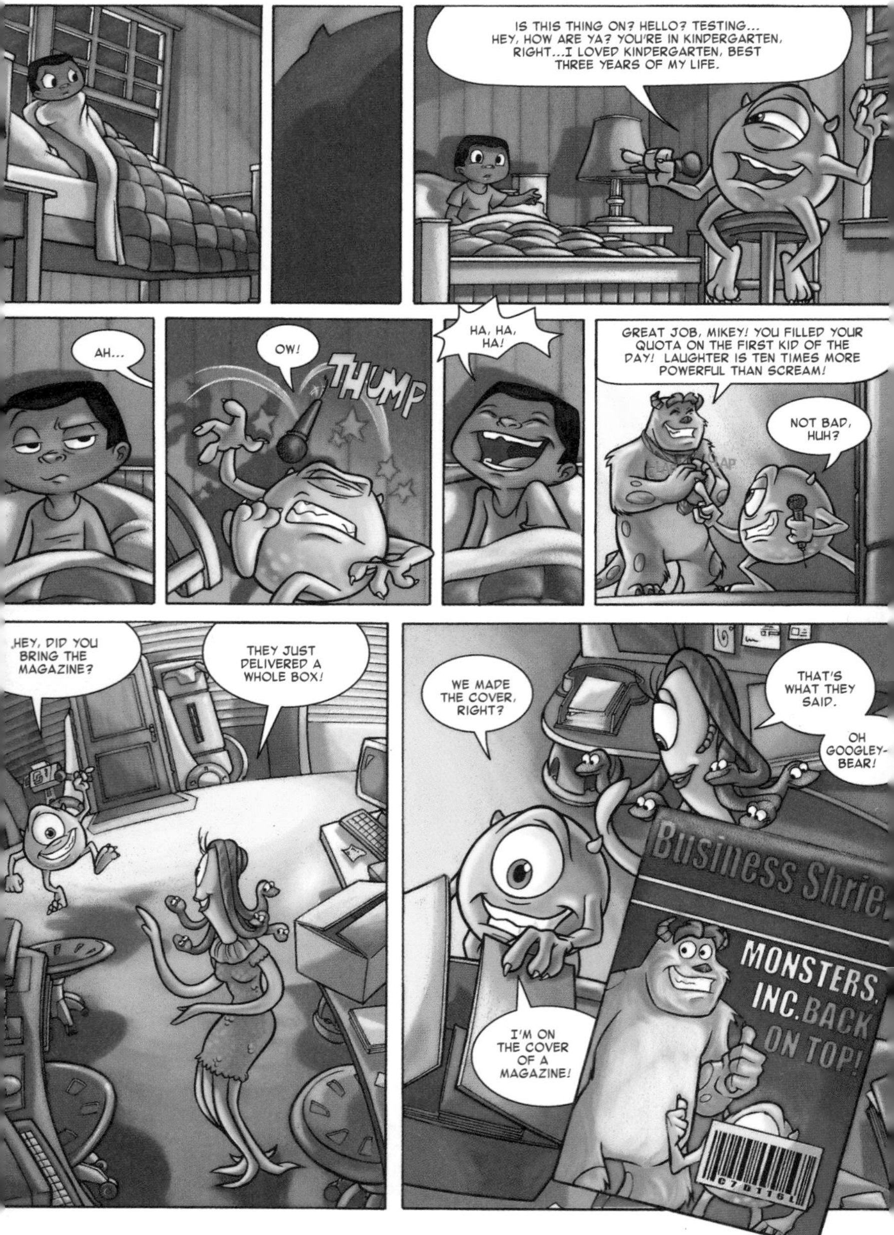
IS THIS THING ON? HELLO? TESTING... HEY, HOW ARE YA? YOU'RE IN KINDERGARTEN, RIGHT...I LOVED KINDERGARTEN, BEST THREE YEARS OF MY LIFE.
AH...
OW!
THUMP
HA, HA, HA!
GREAT JOB, MIKEY! YOU FILLED YOUR QUOTA ON THE FIRST KID OF THE DAY! LAUGHTER IS TEN TIMES MORE POWERFUL THAN SCREAM!
NOT BAD, HUH?
HEY, DID YOU BRING THE MAGAZINE?
THEY JUST DELIVERED A WHOLE BOX!
WE MADE THE COVER, RIGHT?
THAT'S WHAT THEY SAID.
OH GOOGLEY-BEAR!
Business Shrie
MONSTERS, INC. BACK ON TOP!
I'M ON THE COVER OF A MAGAZINE!

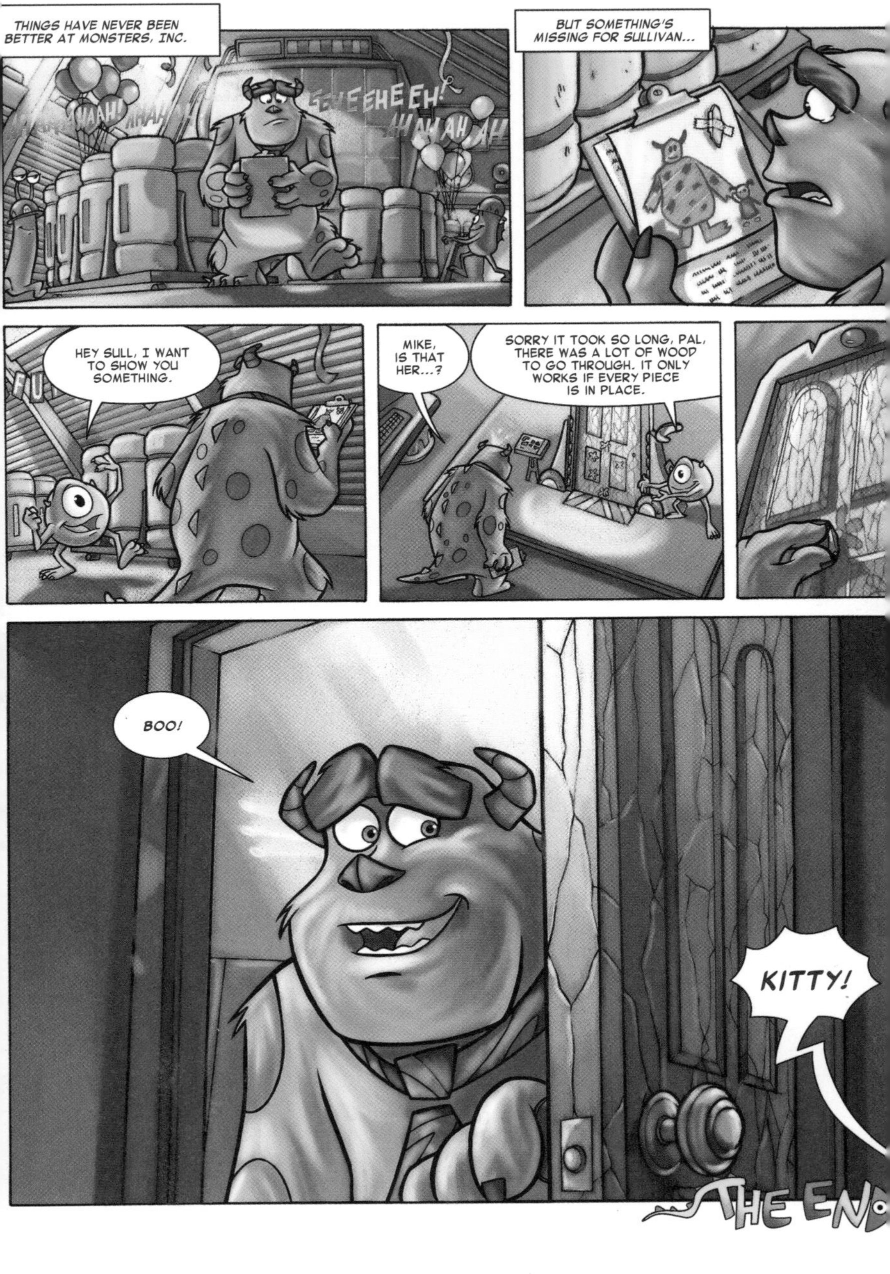

THINGS HAVE NEVER BEEN BETTER AT MONSTERS, INC.
BUT SOMETHING'S MISSING FOR SULLIVAN...
HEY SULL, I WANT TO SHOW YOU SOMETHING.
MIKE, IS THAT HER...?
SORRY IT TOOK SO LONG, PAL, THERE WAS A LOT OF WOOD TO GO THROUGH. IT ONLY WORKS IF EVERY PIECE IS IN PLACE.
BOO!
KITTY!
THE END

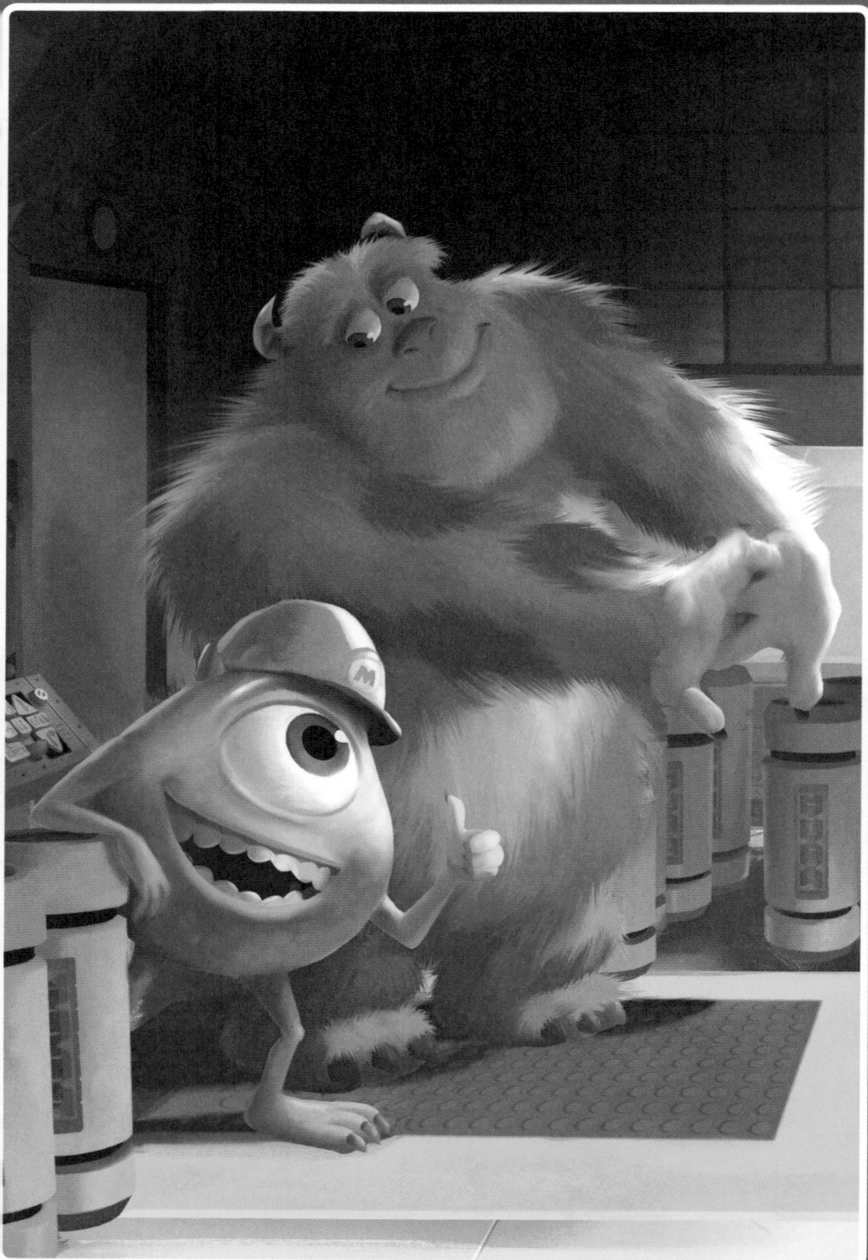

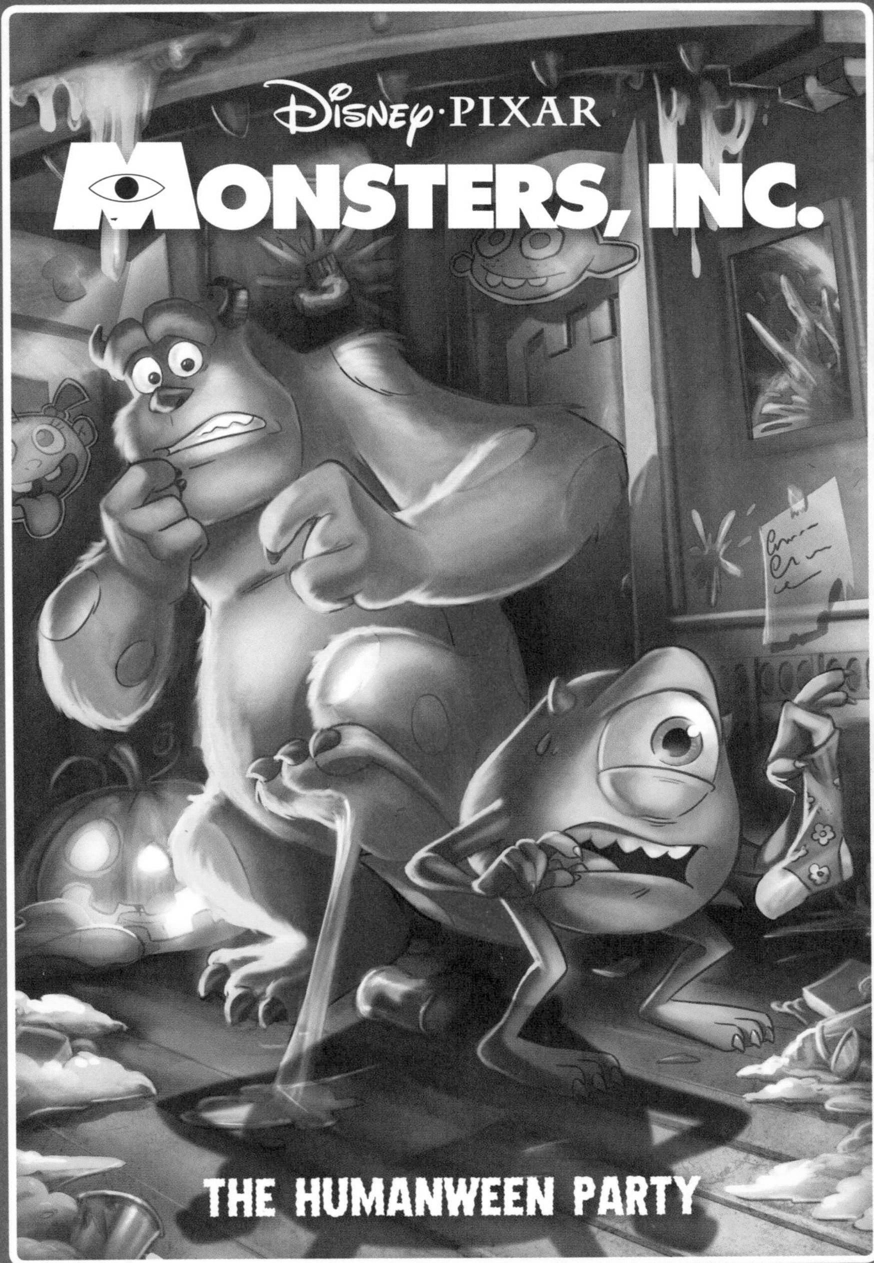
DISNEY·PIXAR
MONSTERS, INC.
THE HUMANWEEN PARTY

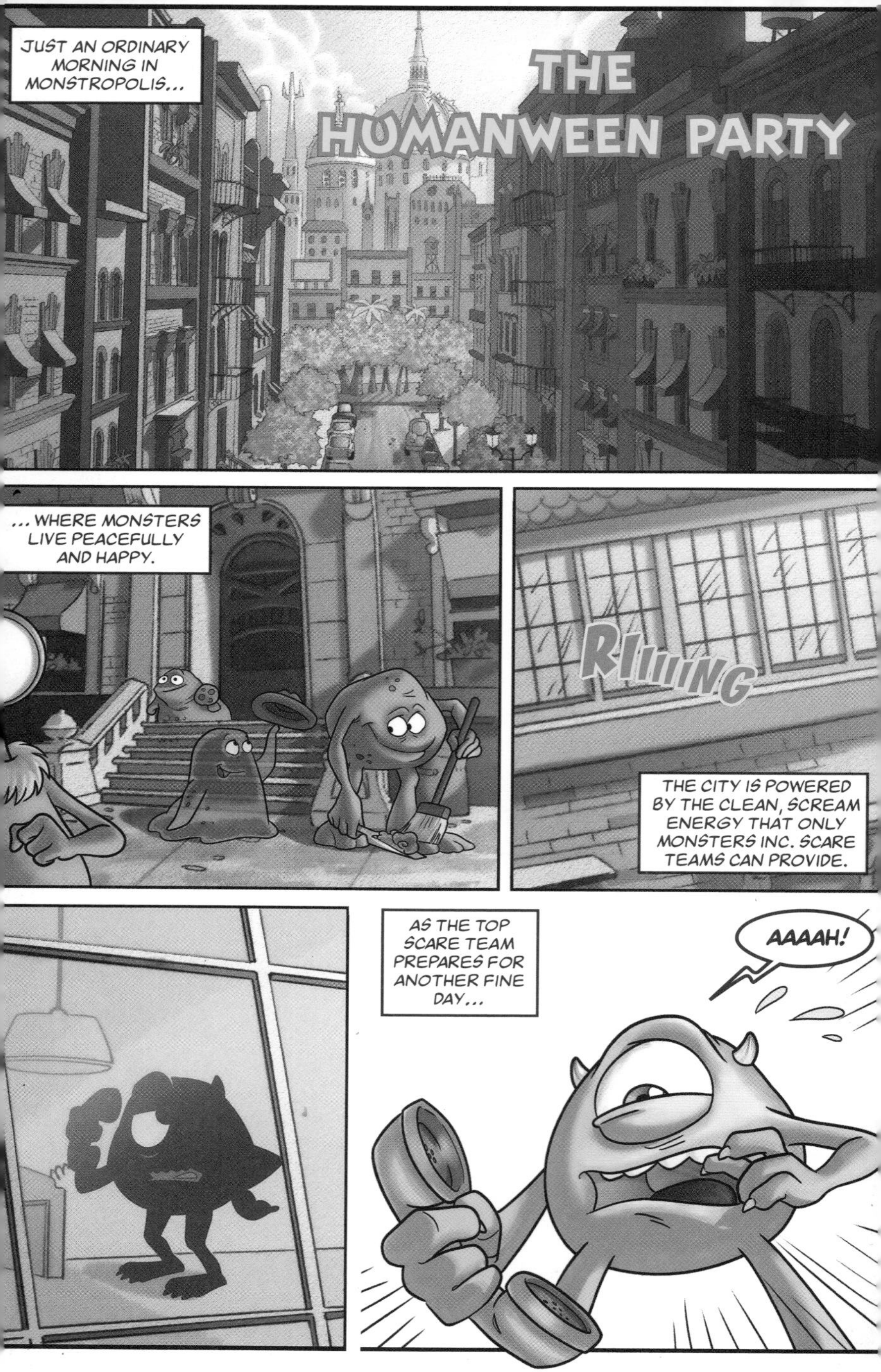

JUST AN ORDINARY MORNING IN MONSTROPOLIS...
THE HUMANWEEN PARTY
... WHERE MONSTERS LIVE PEACEFULLY AND HAPPY.
RIIIIING
THE CITY IS POWERED BY THE CLEAN, SCREAM ENERGY THAT ONLY MONSTERS INC. SCARE TEAMS CAN PROVIDE.
AS THE TOP SCARE TEAM PREPARES FOR ANOTHER FINE DAY...
AAAAH!

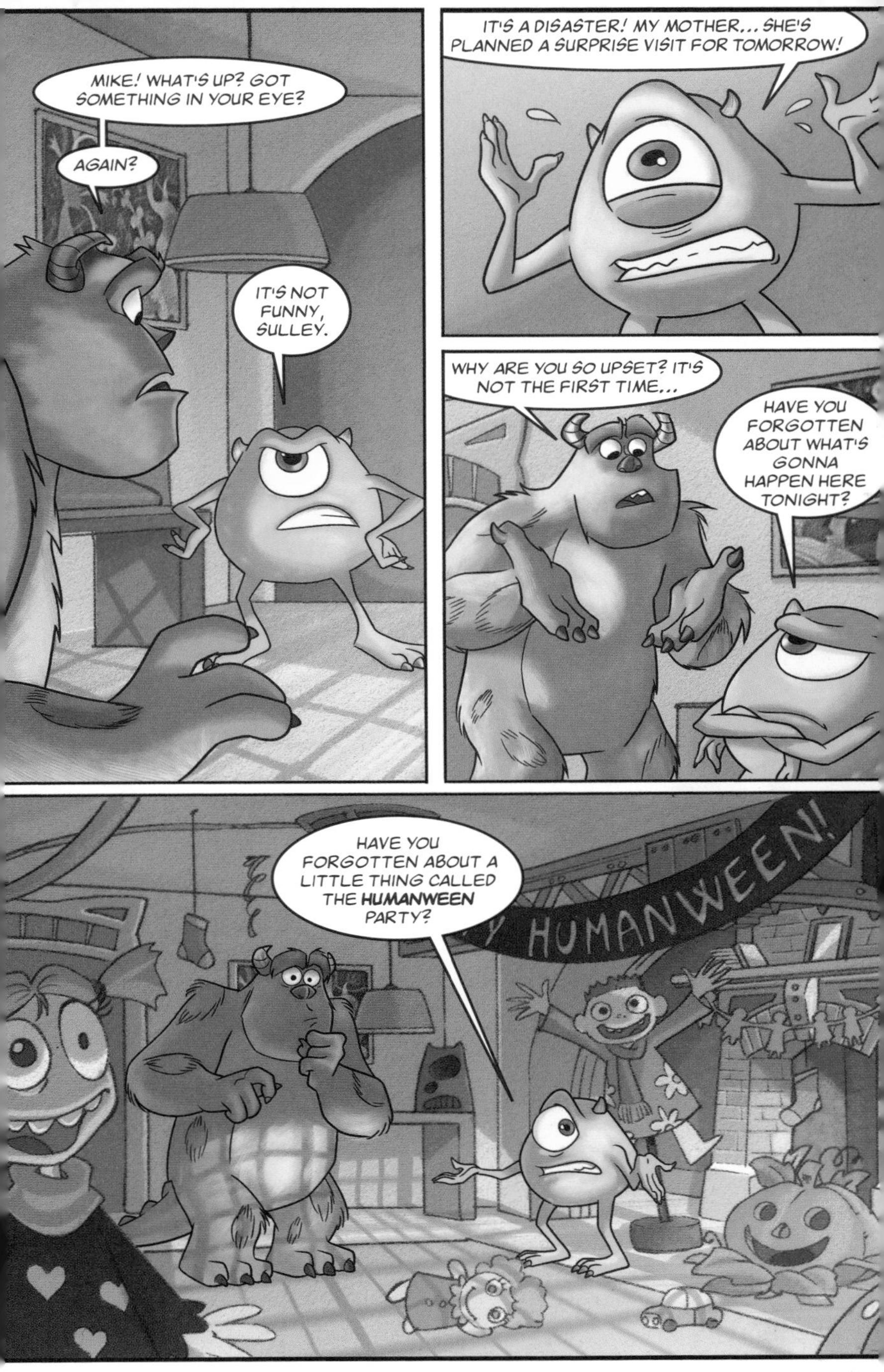
MIKE! WHAT'S UP? GOT SOMETHING IN YOUR EYE?
AGAIN?
IT'S NOT FUNNY, SULLEY.
IT'S A DISASTER! MY MOTHER... SHE'S PLANNED A SURPRISE VISIT FOR TOMORROW!
WHY ARE YOU SO UPSET? IT'S NOT THE FIRST TIME...
HAVE YOU FORGOTTEN ABOUT WHAT'S GONNA HAPPEN HERE TONIGHT?
HAVE YOU FORGOTTEN ABOUT A LITTLE THING CALLED THE **HUMANWEEN** PARTY?
HUMANWEEN!

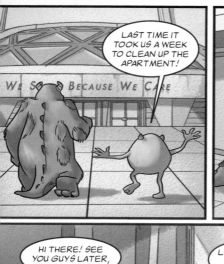

LAST TIME IT TOOK US A WEEK TO CLEAN UP THE APARTMENT!

WE SO... BECAUSE WE CARE

I DON'T WANT MY MOM TO SEE HOW MESSY THE PLACE WILL BE. SHE'LL THINK WE LIVE IN A DUMP!

MAYBE NO ONE'S GONNA COME...

HI THERE! SEE YOU GUYS LATER, SULLEY?

LIKE EVERY YEAR, RICKY!

SULLIVAN! WAZOWSKI! MARGE AND I ARE BRINGING THE SLIMY SLIDE!

PERFECT!

TO SCAREDOORS

TO SCAREFL...

I'M BRINGING MY COUSIN TONIGHT. ALL SEVEN OF HIS HEADS ARE READY TO PARTY!

SURE, JERRY!

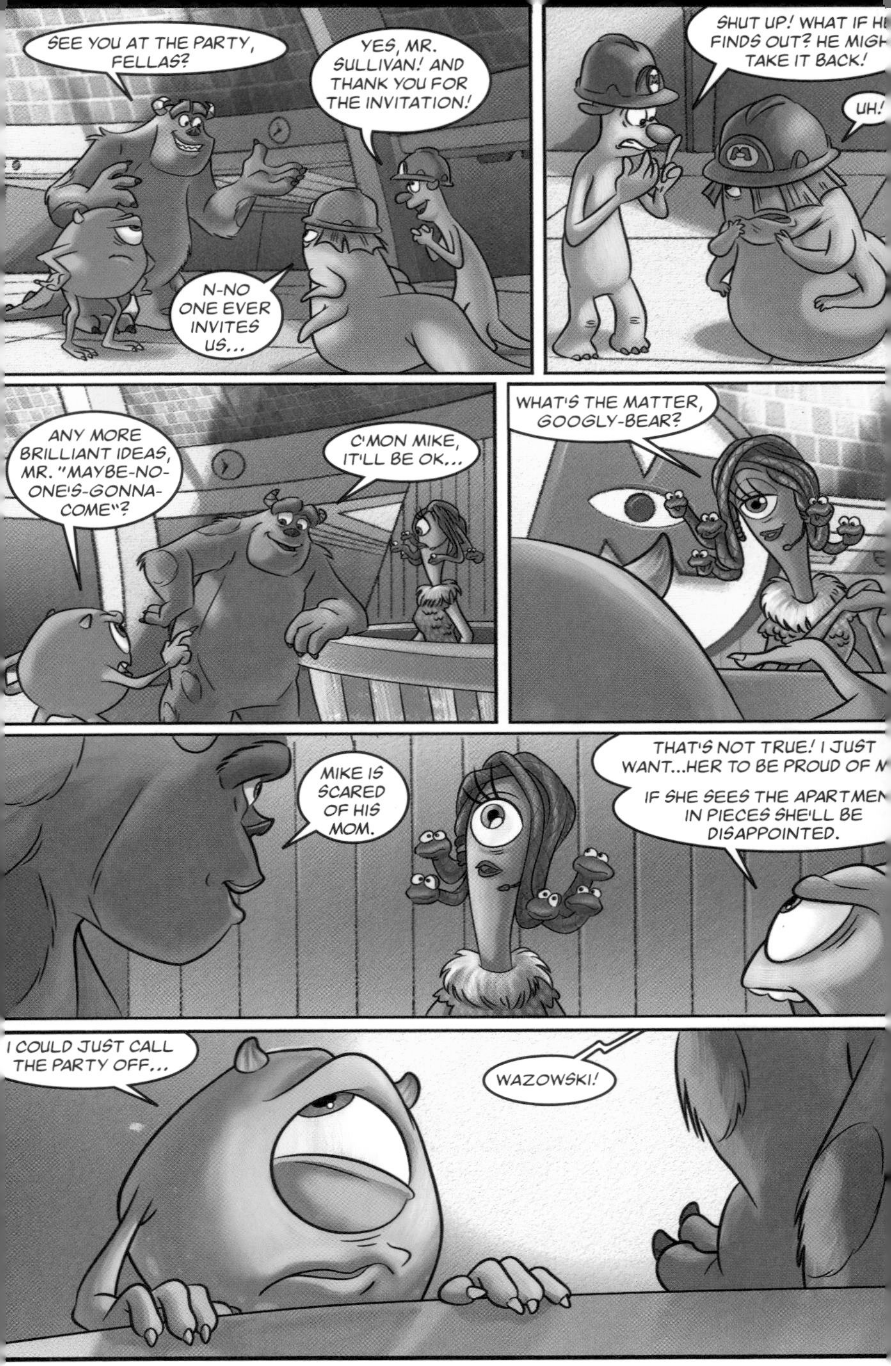
SEE YOU AT THE PARTY, FELLAS?
YES, MR. SULLIVAN! AND THANK YOU FOR THE INVITATION!
N-NO ONE EVER INVITES US...
SHUT UP! WHAT IF HE FINDS OUT? HE MIGH TAKE IT BACK!
UH!
ANY MORE BRILLIANT IDEAS, MR. "MAYBE-NO-ONE'S-GONNA-COME"?
C'MON MIKE, IT'LL BE OK...
WHAT'S THE MATTER, GOOGLY-BEAR?
MIKE IS SCARED OF HIS MOM.
THAT'S NOT TRUE! I JUST WANT...HER TO BE PROUD OF M
IF SHE SEES THE APARTMEN IN PIECES SHE'LL BE DISAPPOINTED.
I COULD JUST CALL THE PARTY OFF...
WAZOWSKI!

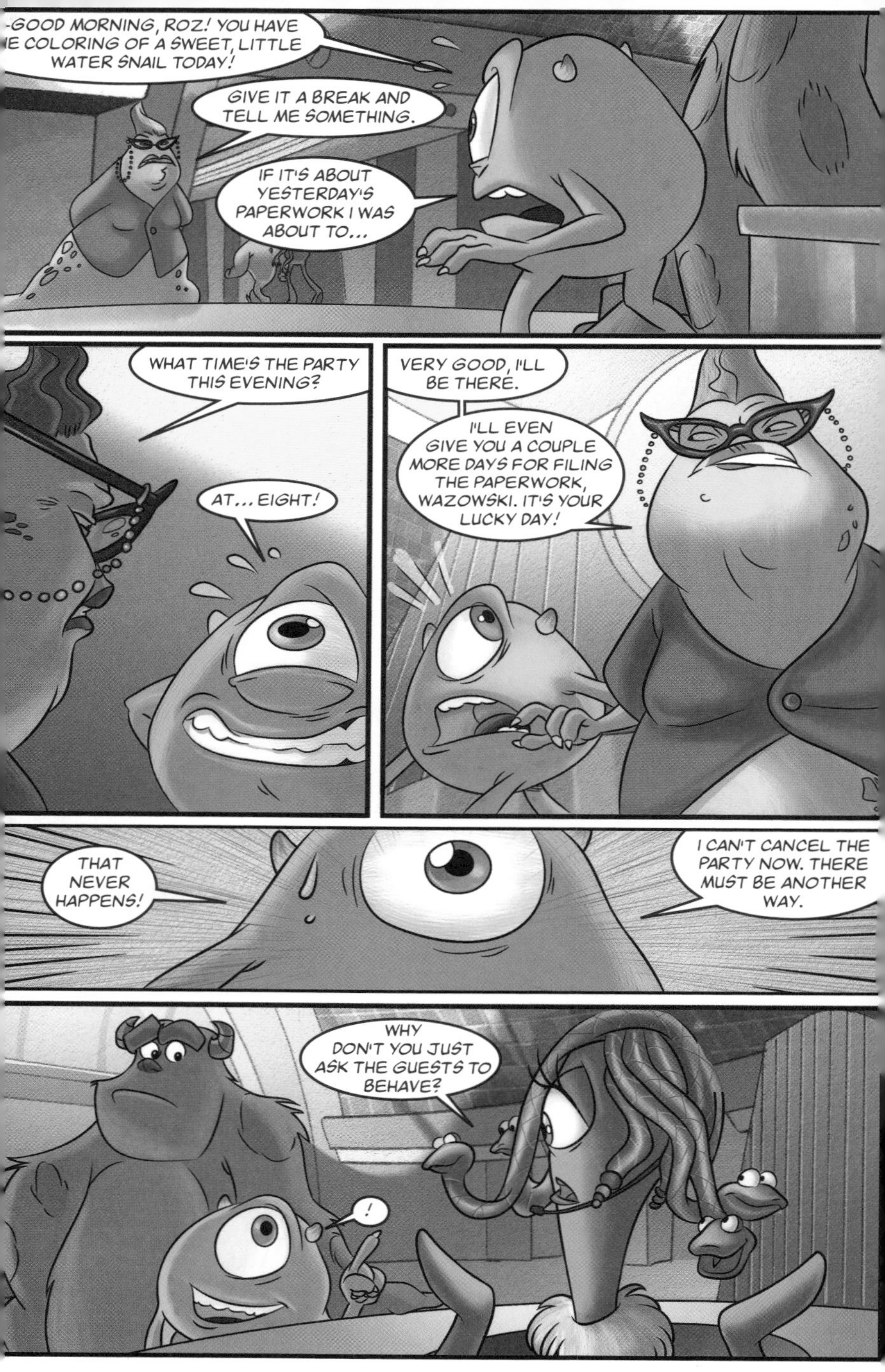
-GOOD MORNING, ROZ! YOU HAVE
E COLORING OF A SWEET, LITTLE WATER SNAIL TODAY!
GIVE IT A BREAK AND TELL ME SOMETHING.
IF IT'S ABOUT YESTERDAY'S PAPERWORK I WAS ABOUT TO...
WHAT TIME'S THE PARTY THIS EVENING?
AT... EIGHT!
VERY GOOD, I'LL BE THERE.
I'LL EVEN GIVE YOU A COUPLE MORE DAYS FOR FILING THE PAPERWORK, WAZOWSKI. IT'S YOUR LUCKY DAY!
THAT NEVER HAPPENS!
I CAN'T CANCEL THE PARTY NOW. THERE MUST BE ANOTHER WAY.
WHY DON'T YOU JUST ASK THE GUESTS TO BEHAVE?
!

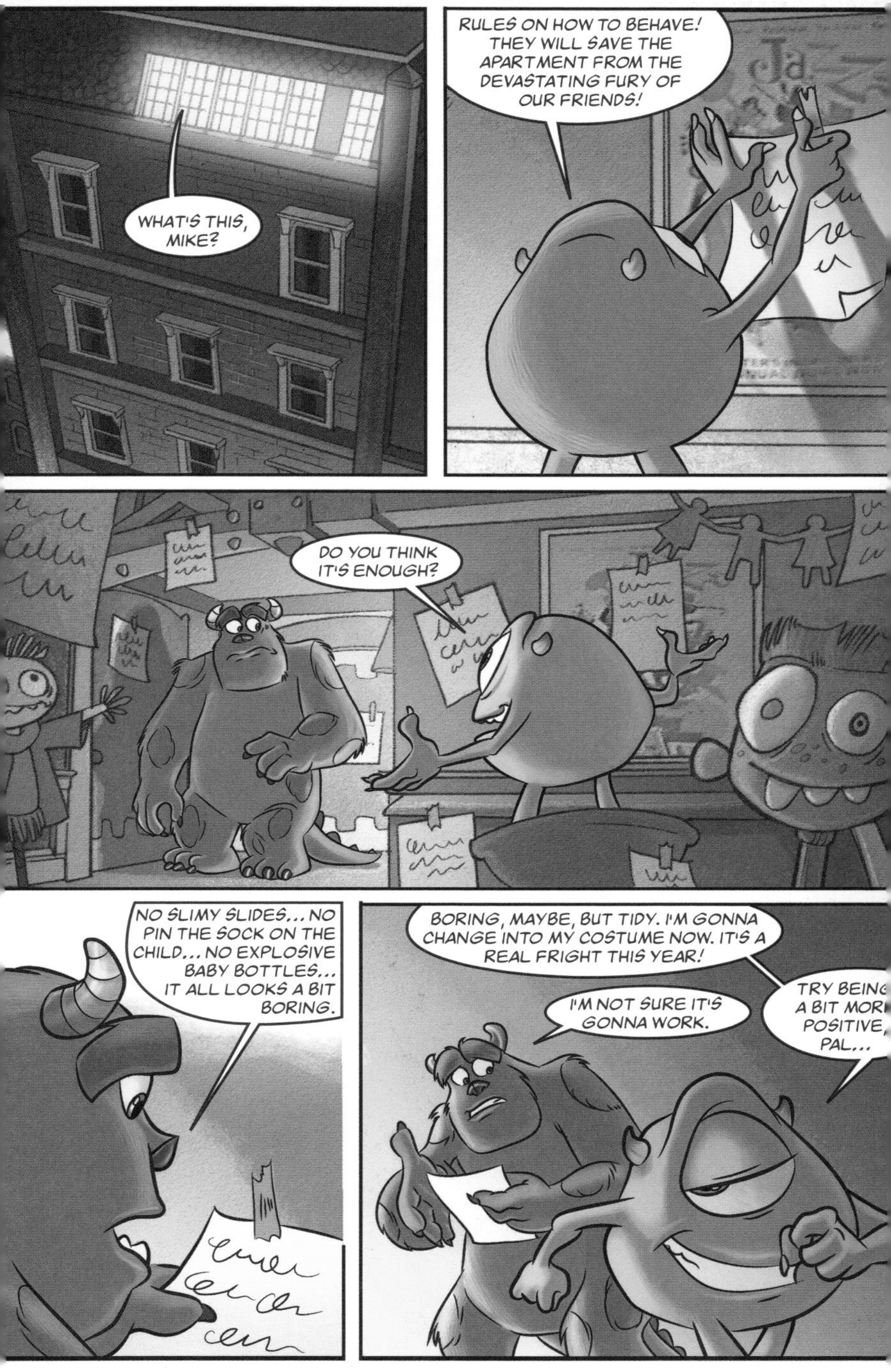
WHAT'S THIS, MIKE?
RULES ON HOW TO BEHAVE! THEY WILL SAVE THE APARTMENT FROM THE DEVASTATING FURY OF OUR FRIENDS!
DO YOU THINK IT'S ENOUGH?
NO SLIMY SLIDES... NO PIN THE SOCK ON THE CHILD... NO EXPLOSIVE BABY BOTTLES... IT ALL LOOKS A BIT BORING.
BORING, MAYBE, BUT TIDY. I'M GONNA CHANGE INTO MY COSTUME NOW. IT'S A REAL FRIGHT THIS YEAR!
I'M NOT SURE IT'S GONNA WORK.
TRY BEING A BIT MORE POSITIVE, PAL...

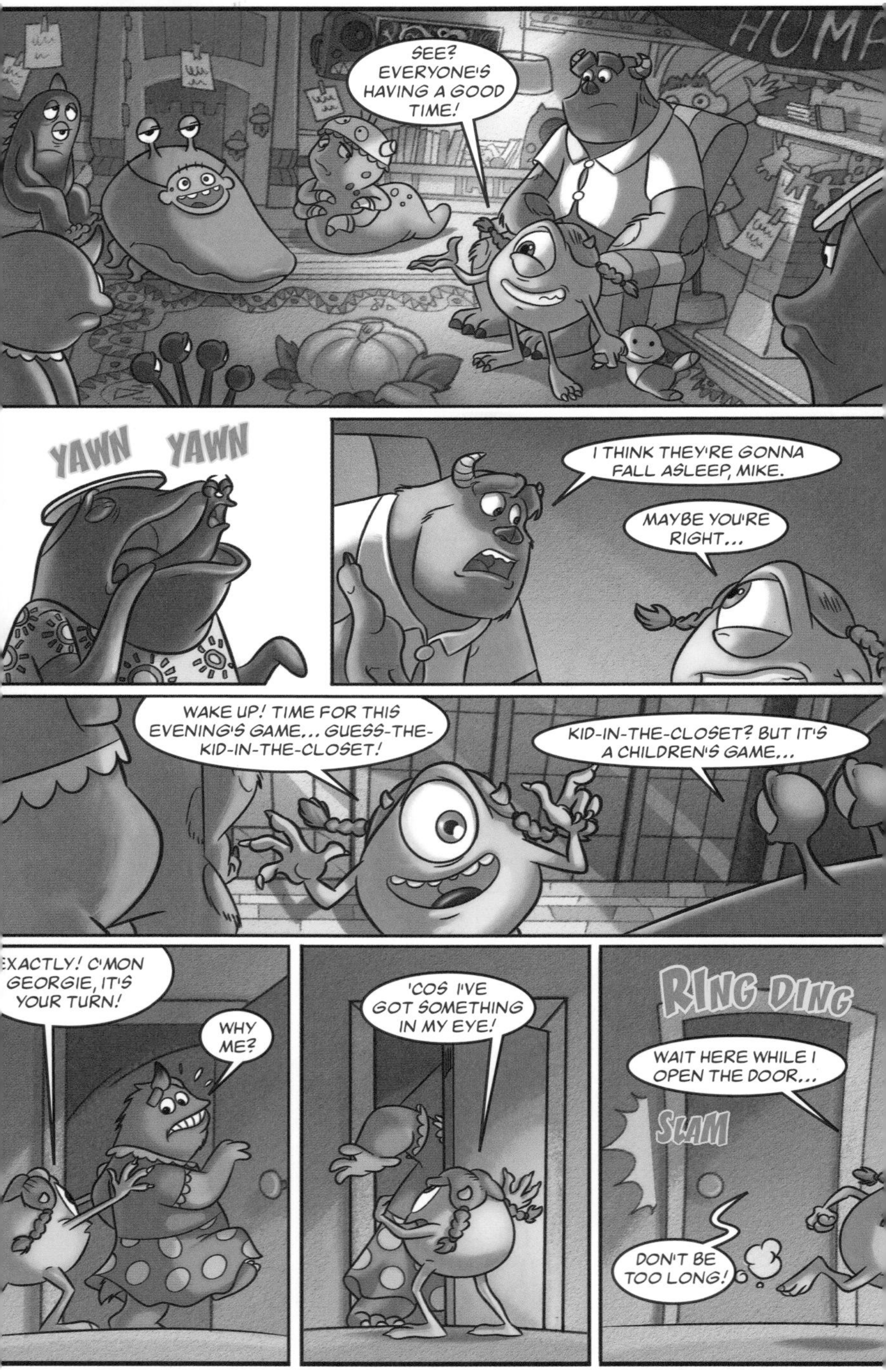

SEE? EVERYONE'S HAVING A GOOD TIME!
HOM
YAWN YAWN
I THINK THEY'RE GONNA FALL ASLEEP, MIKE.
MAYBE YOU'RE RIGHT...
WAKE UP! TIME FOR THIS EVENING'S GAME... GUESS-THE-KID-IN-THE-CLOSET!
KID-IN-THE-CLOSET? BUT IT'S A CHILDREN'S GAME...
EXACTLY! C'MON GEORGIE, IT'S YOUR TURN!
WHY ME?
'COS I'VE GOT SOMETHING IN MY EYE!
RING DING
WAIT HERE WHILE I OPEN THE DOOR...
SLAM
DON'T BE TOO LONG!

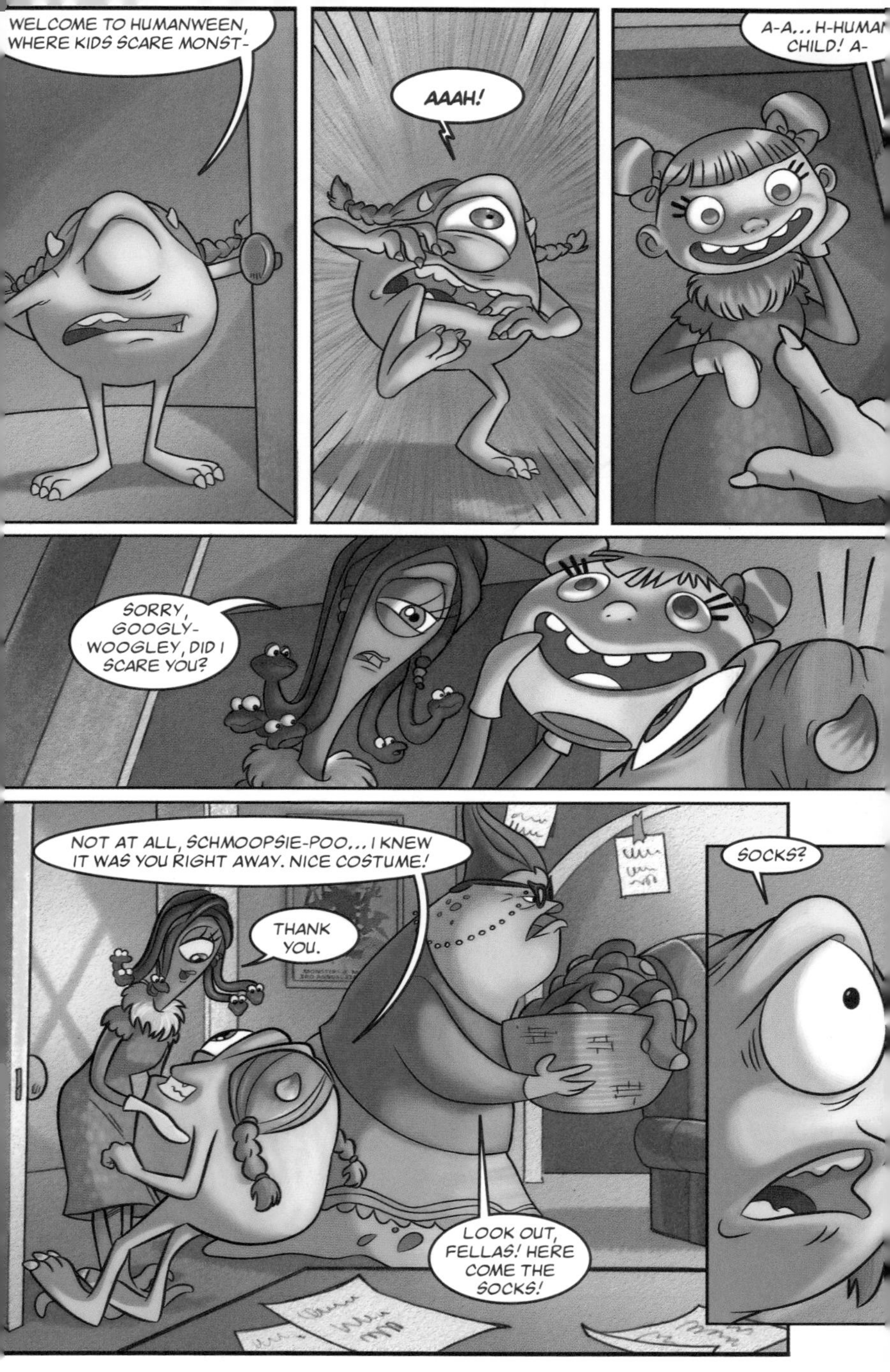

WELCOME TO HUMANWEEN, WHERE KIDS SCARE MONST-
AAAH!
A-A... H-HUMAN CHILD! A-
SORRY, GOOGLY-WOOGLEY, DID I SCARE YOU?
NOT AT ALL, SCHMOOPSIE-POO... I KNEW IT WAS YOU RIGHT AWAY. NICE COSTUME!
THANK YOU.
LOOK OUT, FELLAS! HERE COME THE SOCKS!
SOCKS?

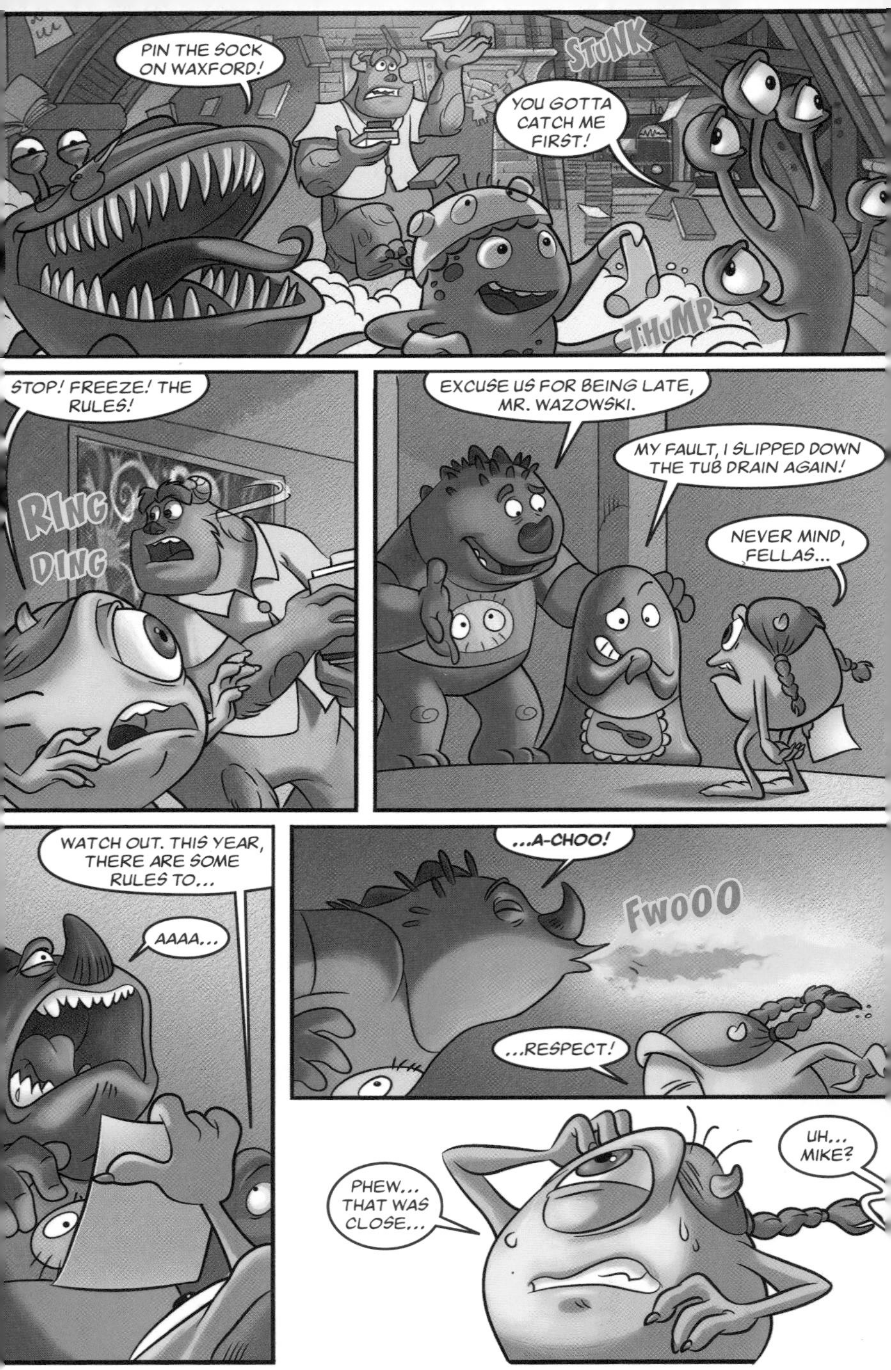
PIN THE SOCK ON WAXFORD!
STUNK
YOU GOTTA CATCH ME FIRST!
THUMP
STOP! FREEZE! THE RULES!
RING
DING
EXCUSE US FOR BEING LATE, MR. WAZOWSKI.
MY FAULT, I SLIPPED DOWN THE TUB DRAIN AGAIN!
NEVER MIND, FELLAS...
WATCH OUT. THIS YEAR, THERE ARE SOME RULES TO...
AAAA...
...A-CHOO!
FWOOO
...RESPECT!
PHEW... THAT WAS CLOSE...
UH... MIKE?

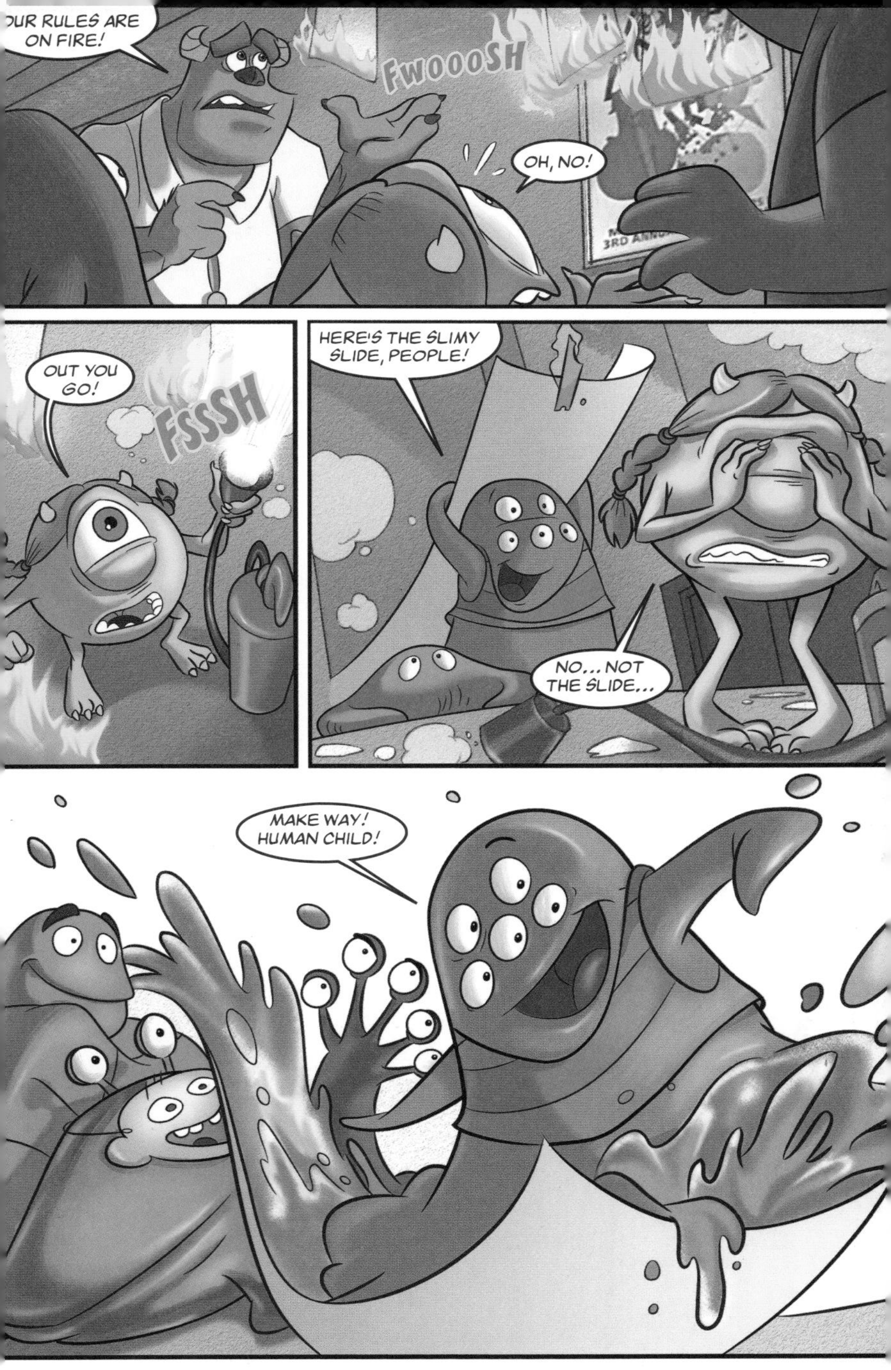
OUR RULES ARE ON FIRE!
FWOOOOSH
OH, NO!
MI 3RD ANN
OUT YOU GO!
FSSSH
HERE'S THE SLIMY SLIDE, PEOPLE!
NO... NOT THE SLIDE...
MAKE WAY! HUMAN CHILD!

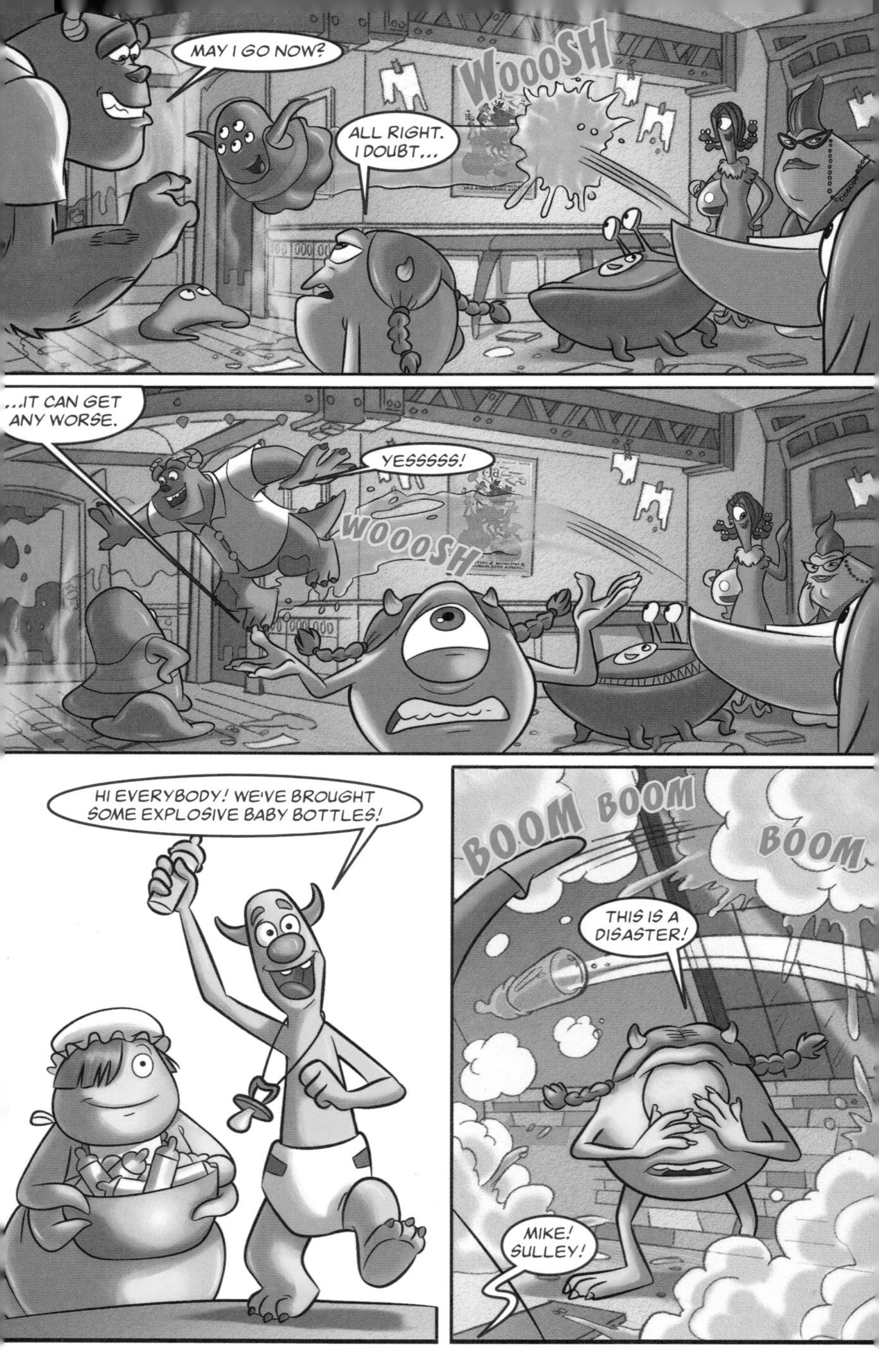
MAY I GO NOW?
WOOOSH
ALL RIGHT. I DOUBT...
...IT CAN GET ANY WORSE.
YESSSSS!
WOOOSH
HI EVERYBODY! WE'VE BROUGHT SOME EXPLOSIVE BABY BOTTLES!
BOOM BOOM
BOOM
THIS IS A DISASTER!
MIKE! SULLEY!

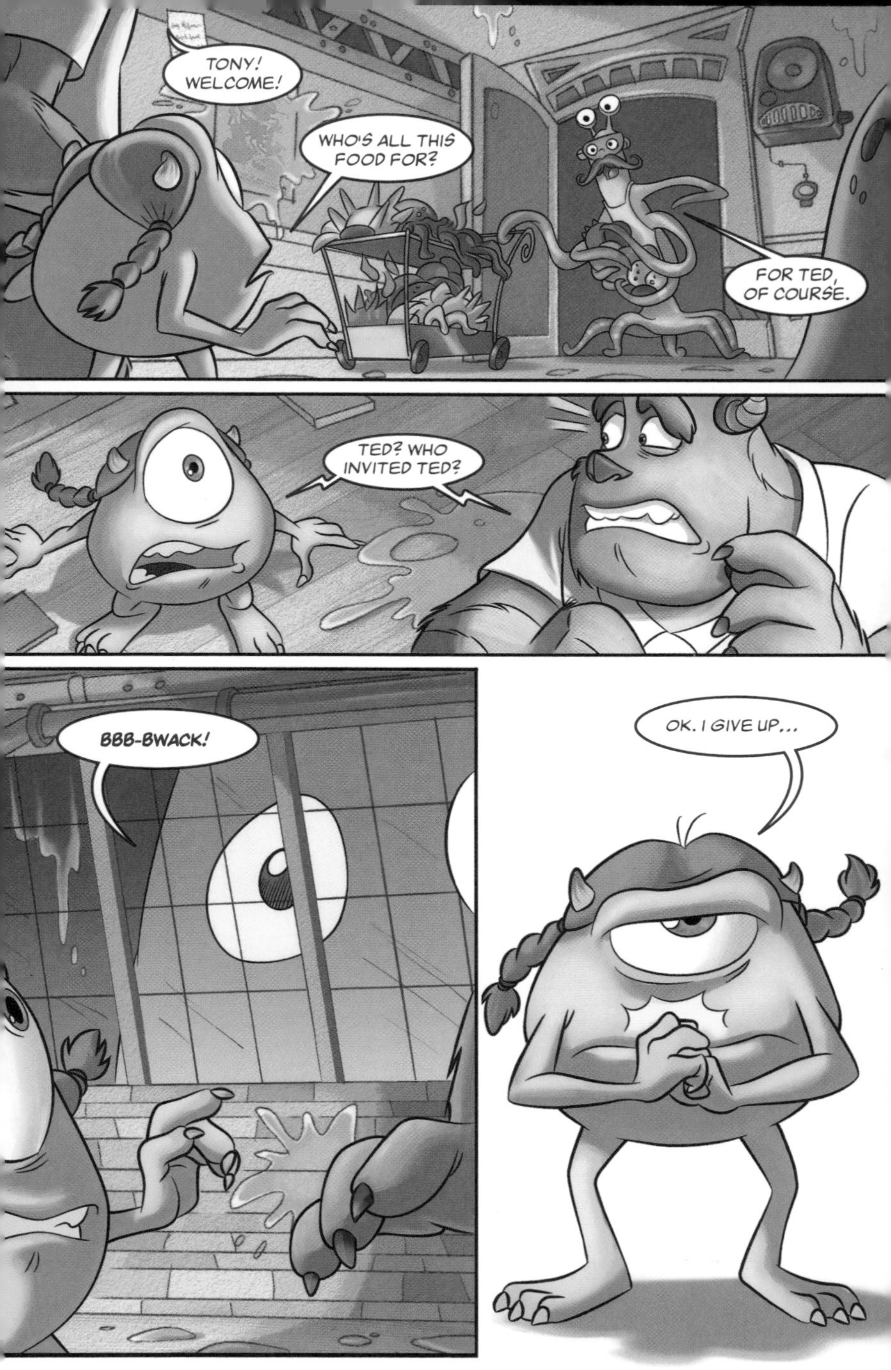
TONY! WELCOME!
WHO'S ALL THIS FOOD FOR?
FOR TED, OF COURSE.
TED? WHO INVITED TED?
BBB-BWACK!
OK. I GIVE UP...

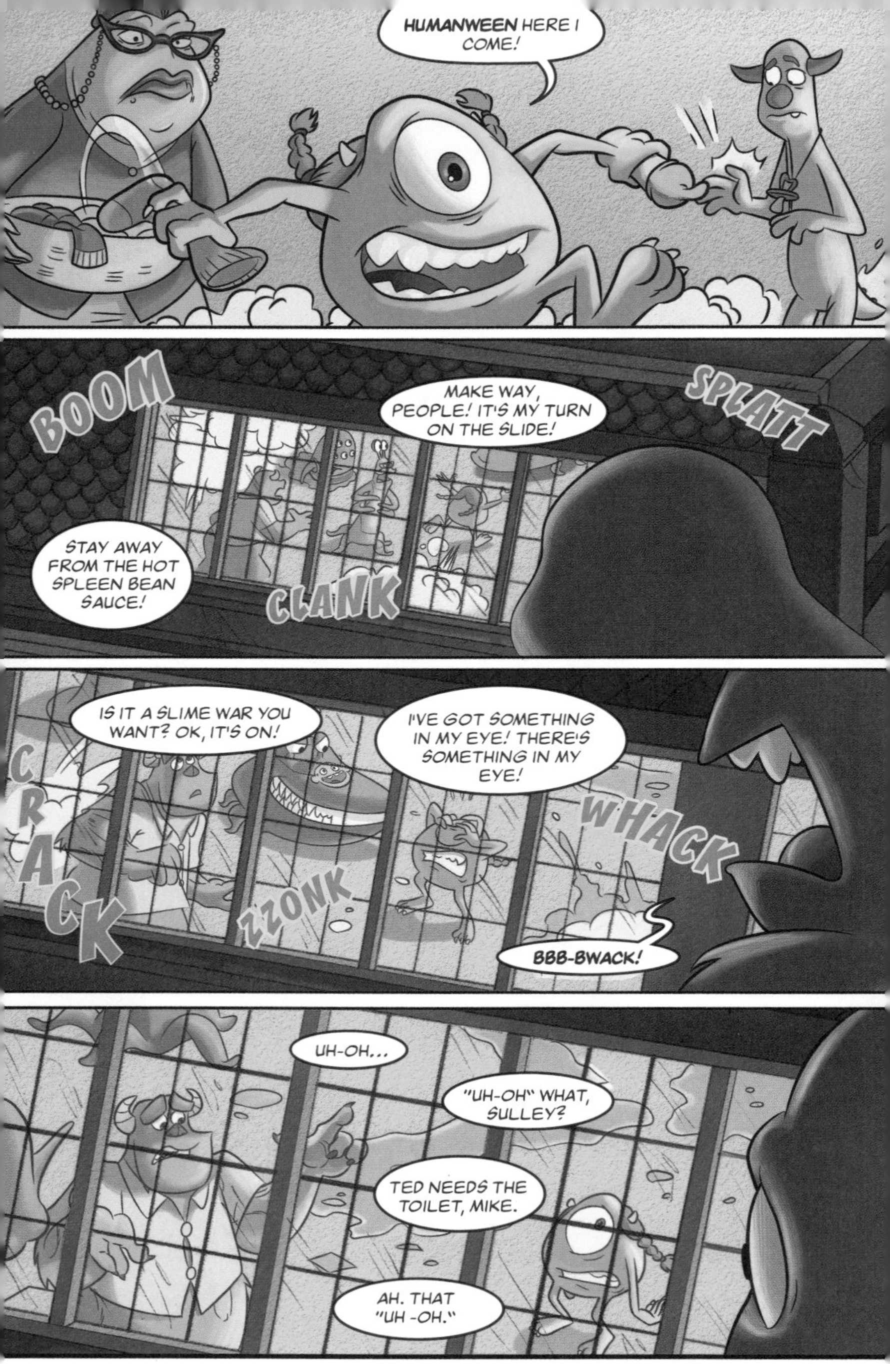
HUMANWEEN HERE I COME!
BOOM
MAKE WAY, PEOPLE! IT'S MY TURN ON THE SLIDE!
SPLATT
STAY AWAY FROM THE HOT SPLEEN BEAN SAUCE!
CLANK
IS IT A SLIME WAR YOU WANT? OK, IT'S ON!
I'VE GOT SOMETHING IN MY EYE! THERE'S SOMETHING IN MY EYE!
CRACK
ZZONK
WHACK
BBB-BWACK!
UH-OH...
"UH-OH" WHAT, SULLEY?
TED NEEDS THE TOILET, MIKE.
AH. THAT "UH -OH."

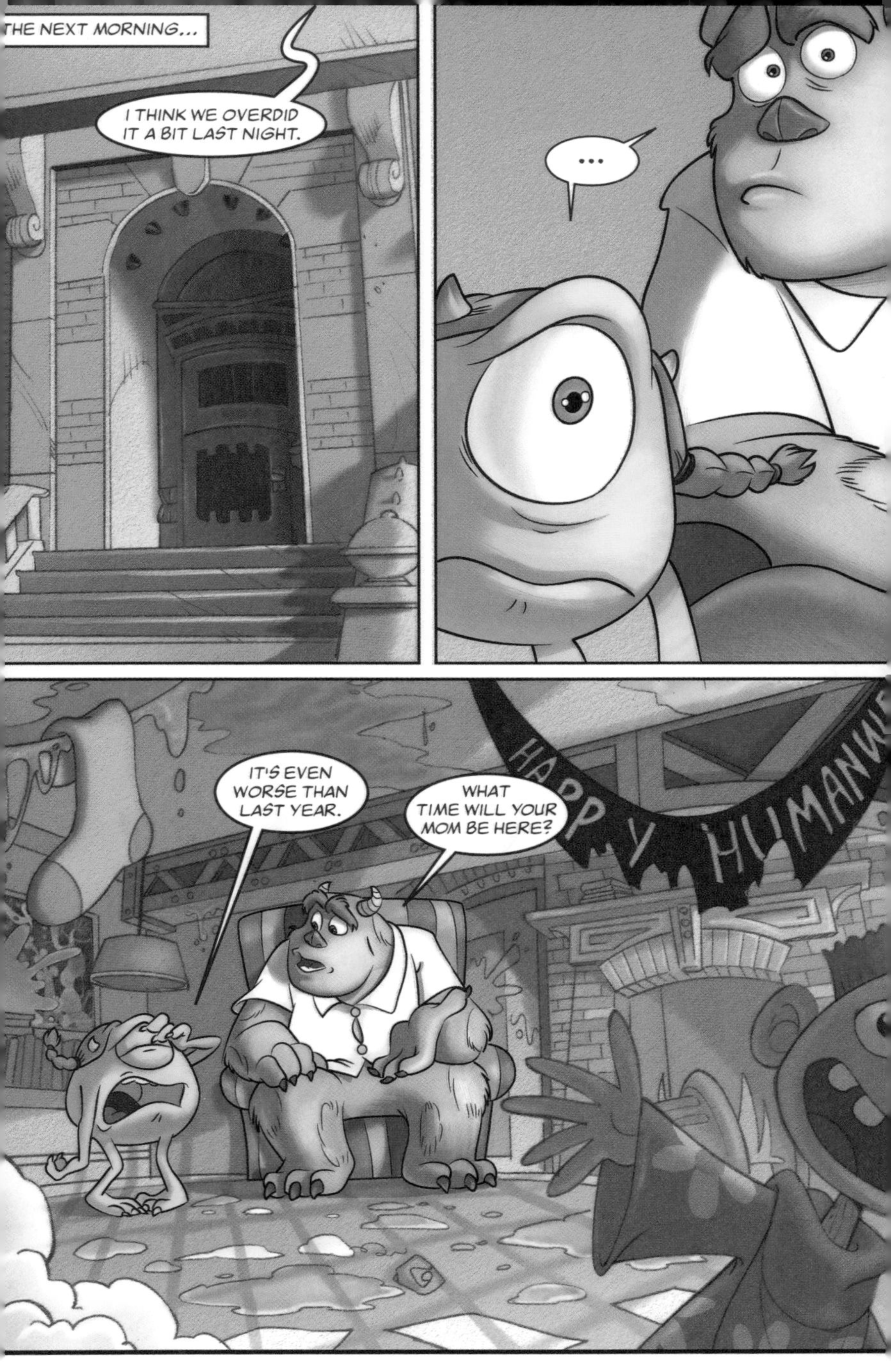
THE NEXT MORNING...
I THINK WE OVERDID IT A BIT LAST NIGHT.
...
IT'S EVEN WORSE THAN LAST YEAR.
WHAT TIME WILL YOUR MOM BE HERE?
HAPPY HUMANW

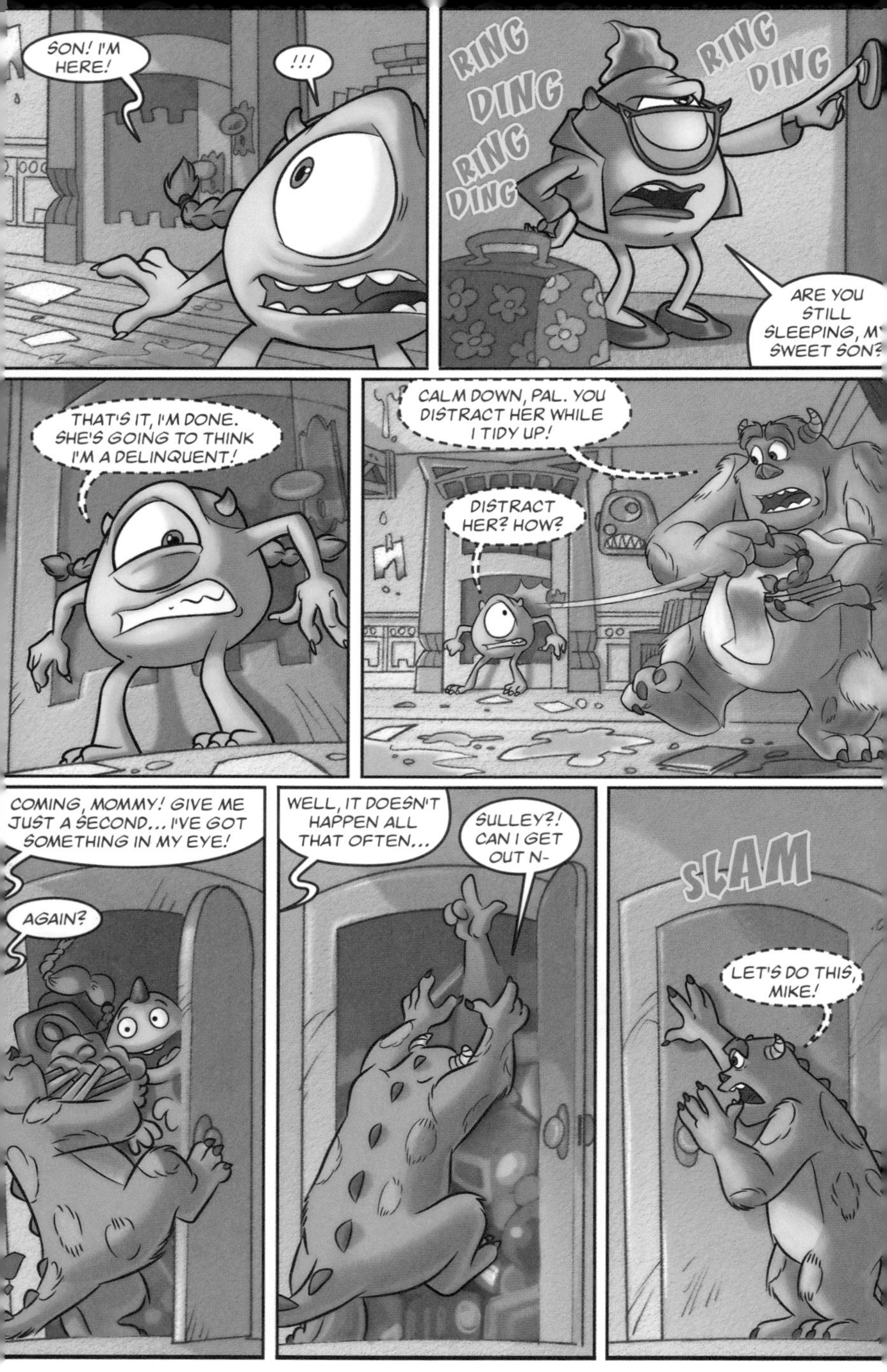
SON! I'M HERE!
!!!
RING
DING
RING
DING
RING
DING
ARE YOU STILL SLEEPING, MY SWEET SON?
THAT'S IT, I'M DONE. SHE'S GOING TO THINK I'M A DELINQUENT!
CALM DOWN, PAL. YOU DISTRACT HER WHILE I TIDY UP!
DISTRACT HER? HOW?
COMING, MOMMY! GIVE ME JUST A SECOND... I'VE GOT SOMETHING IN MY EYE!
AGAIN?
WELL, IT DOESN'T HAPPEN ALL THAT OFTEN...
SULLEY?! CAN I GET OUT N-
SLAM
LET'S DO THIS, MIKE!

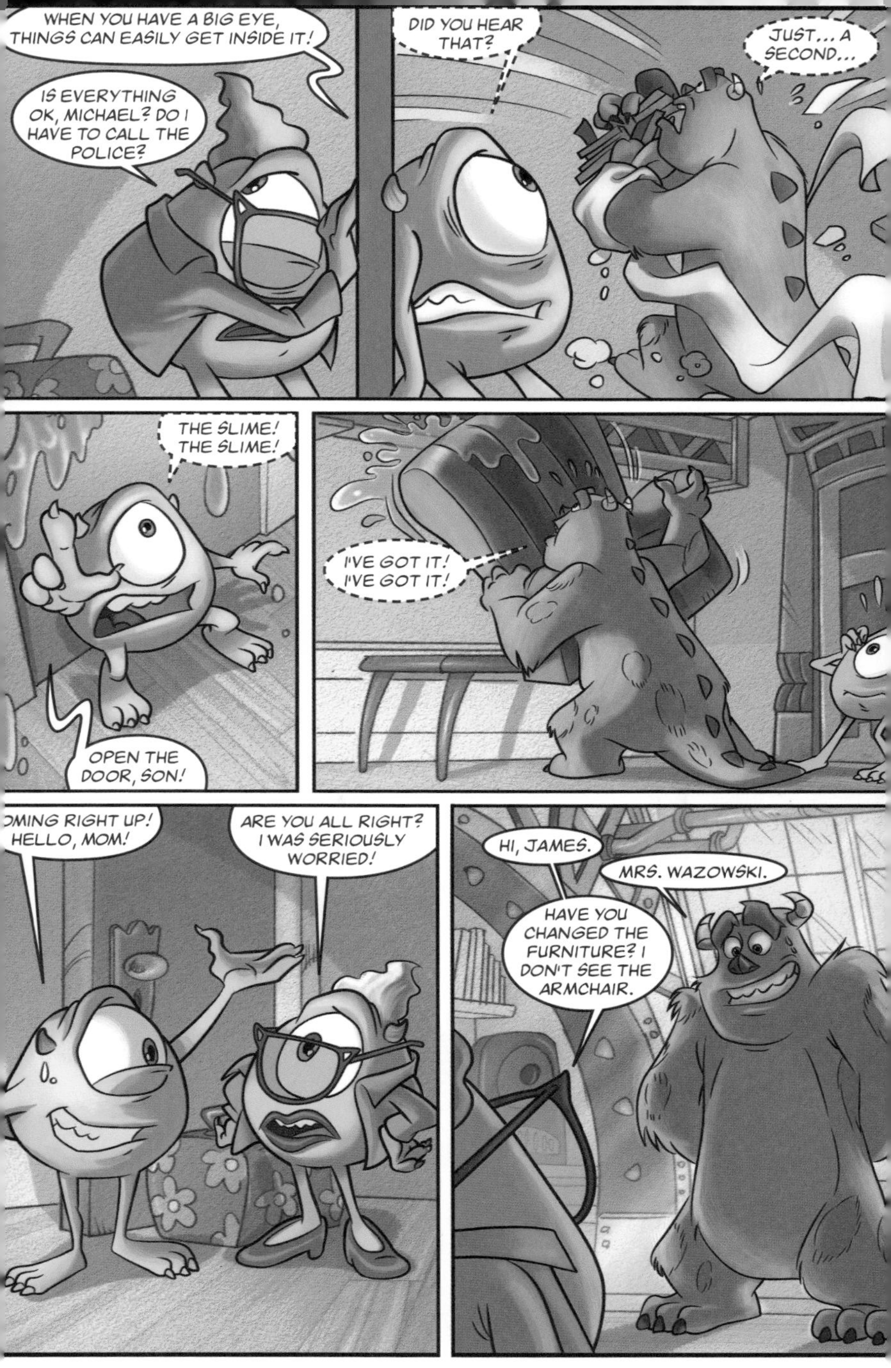
WHEN YOU HAVE A BIG EYE, THINGS CAN EASILY GET INSIDE IT!
IS EVERYTHING OK, MICHAEL? DO I HAVE TO CALL THE POLICE?
DID YOU HEAR THAT?
JUST... A SECOND...
THE SLIME! THE SLIME!
OPEN THE DOOR, SON!
I'VE GOT IT! I'VE GOT IT!
OMING RIGHT UP! HELLO, MOM!
ARE YOU ALL RIGHT? I WAS SERIOUSLY WORRIED!
HI, JAMES.
MRS. WAZOWSKI.
HAVE YOU CHANGED THE FURNITURE? I DON'T SEE THE ARMCHAIR.

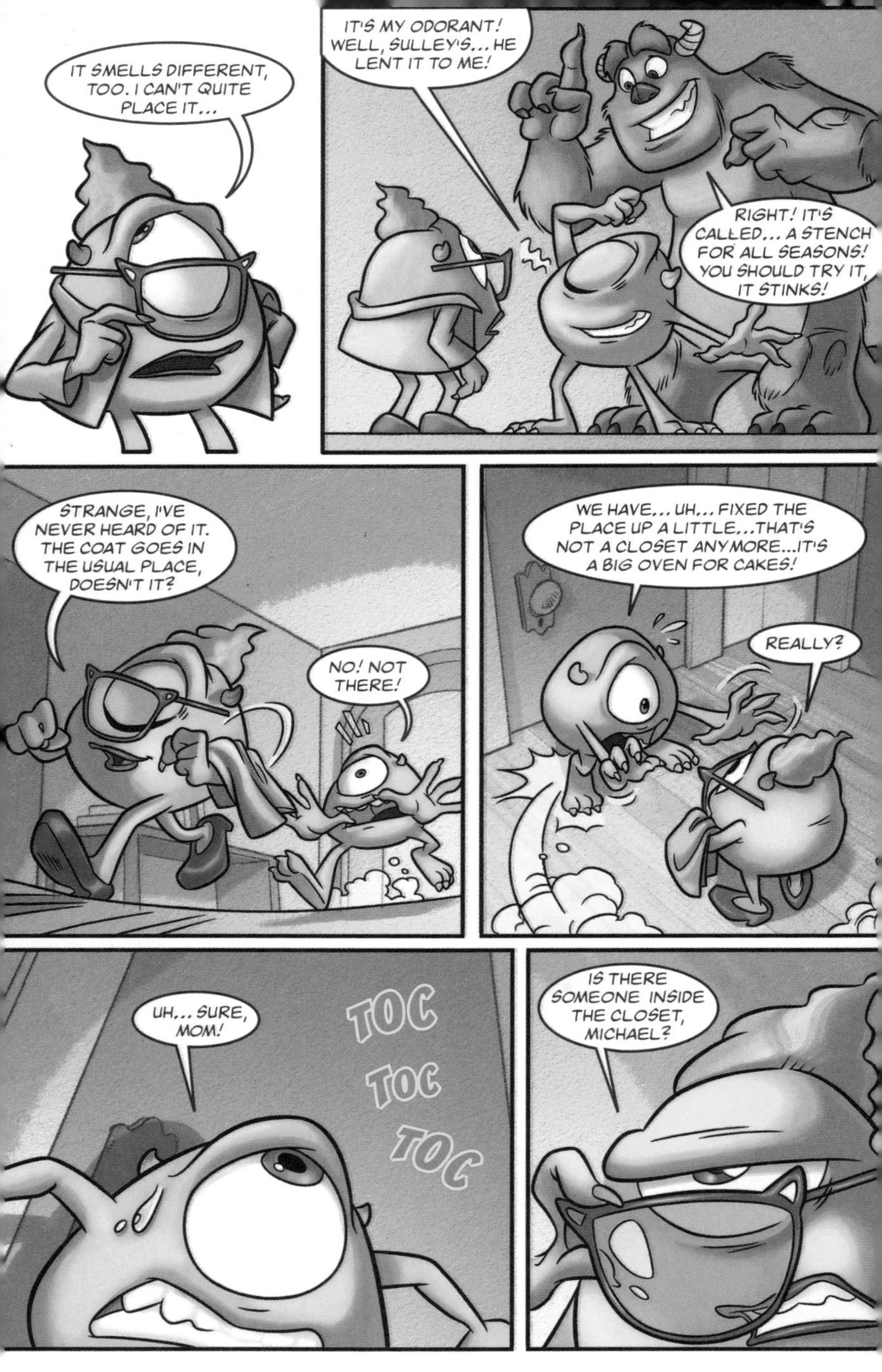
IT SMELLS DIFFERENT, TOO. I CAN'T QUITE PLACE IT...
IT'S MY ODORANT! WELL, SULLEY'S... HE LENT IT TO ME!
RIGHT! IT'S CALLED... A STENCH FOR ALL SEASONS! YOU SHOULD TRY IT, IT STINKS!
STRANGE, I'VE NEVER HEARD OF IT. THE COAT GOES IN THE USUAL PLACE, DOESN'T IT?
NO! NOT THERE!
WE HAVE... UH... FIXED THE PLACE UP A LITTLE... THAT'S NOT A CLOSET ANYMORE... IT'S A BIG OVEN FOR CAKES!
REALLY?
UH... SURE, MOM!
TOC
TOC
TOC
IS THERE SOMEONE INSIDE THE CLOSET, MICHAEL?

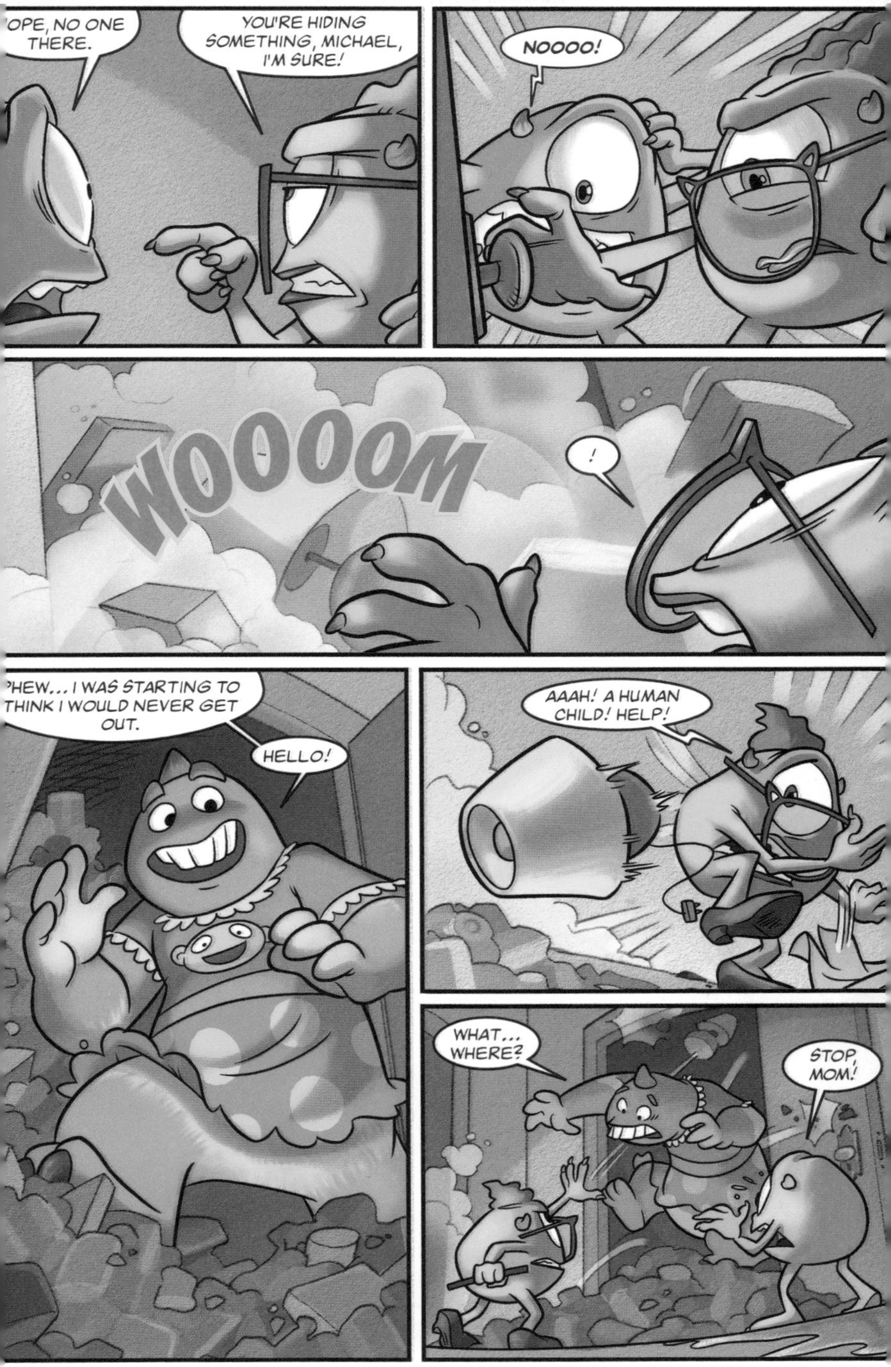

'OPE, NO ONE THERE.
YOU'RE HIDING SOMETHING, MICHAEL, I'M SURE!
NOOOO!
WOOOOM
!
'HEW... I WAS STARTING TO THINK I WOULD NEVER GET OUT.
HELLO!
AAAH! A HUMAN CHILD! HELP!
WHAT... WHERE?
STOP, MOM!

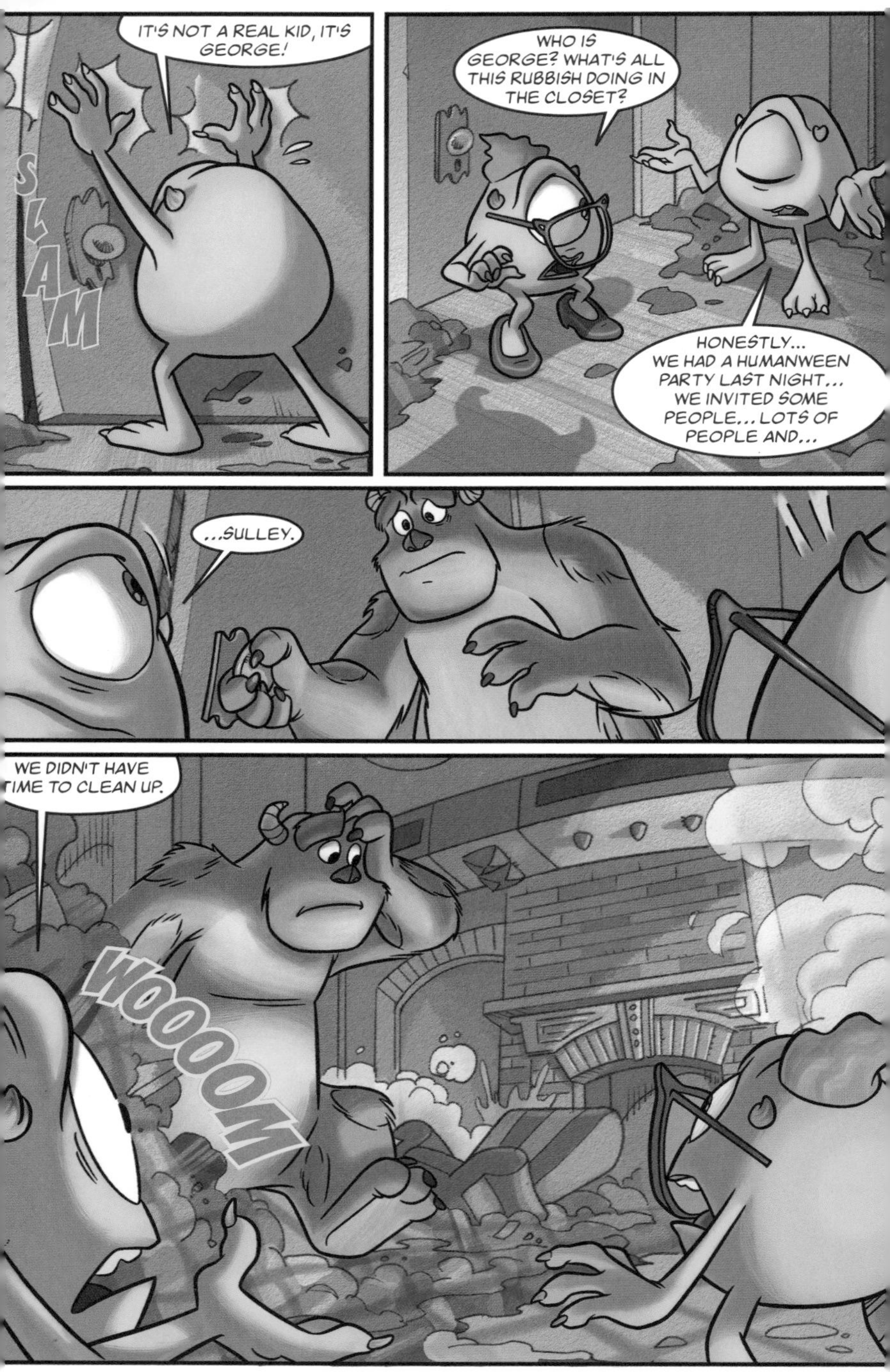
IT'S NOT A REAL KID, IT'S GEORGE!
SLAM
WHO IS GEORGE? WHAT'S ALL THIS RUBBISH DOING IN THE CLOSET?
HONESTLY... WE HAD A HUMANWEEN PARTY LAST NIGHT... WE INVITED SOME PEOPLE... LOTS OF PEOPLE AND...
...SULLEY.
WE DIDN'T HAVE TIME TO CLEAN UP.
WOOOOOM

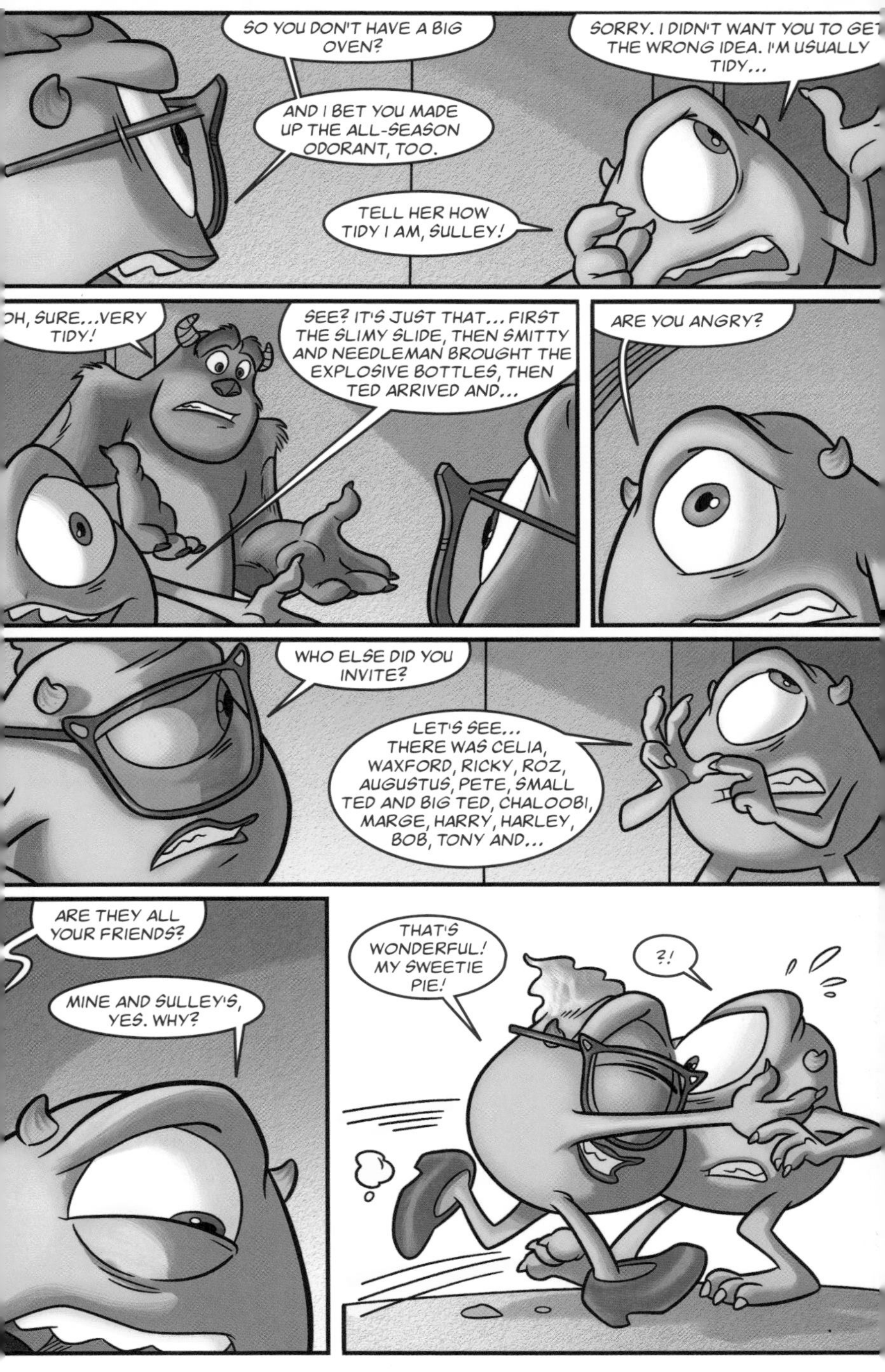
SO YOU DON'T HAVE A BIG OVEN?
AND I BET YOU MADE UP THE ALL-SEASON ODORANT, TOO.
SORRY. I DIDN'T WANT YOU TO GET THE WRONG IDEA. I'M USUALLY TIDY...
TELL HER HOW TIDY I AM, SULLEY!
OH, SURE...VERY TIDY!
SEE? IT'S JUST THAT... FIRST THE SLIMY SLIDE, THEN SMITTY AND NEEDLEMAN BROUGHT THE EXPLOSIVE BOTTLES, THEN TED ARRIVED AND...
ARE YOU ANGRY?
WHO ELSE DID YOU INVITE?
LET'S SEE... THERE WAS CELIA, WAXFORD, RICKY, ROZ, AUGUSTUS, PETE, SMALL TED AND BIG TED, CHALOOBI, MARGE, HARRY, HARLEY, BOB, TONY AND...
ARE THEY ALL YOUR FRIENDS?
MINE AND SULLEY'S, YES. WHY?
THAT'S WONDERFUL! MY SWEETIE PIE!
?!

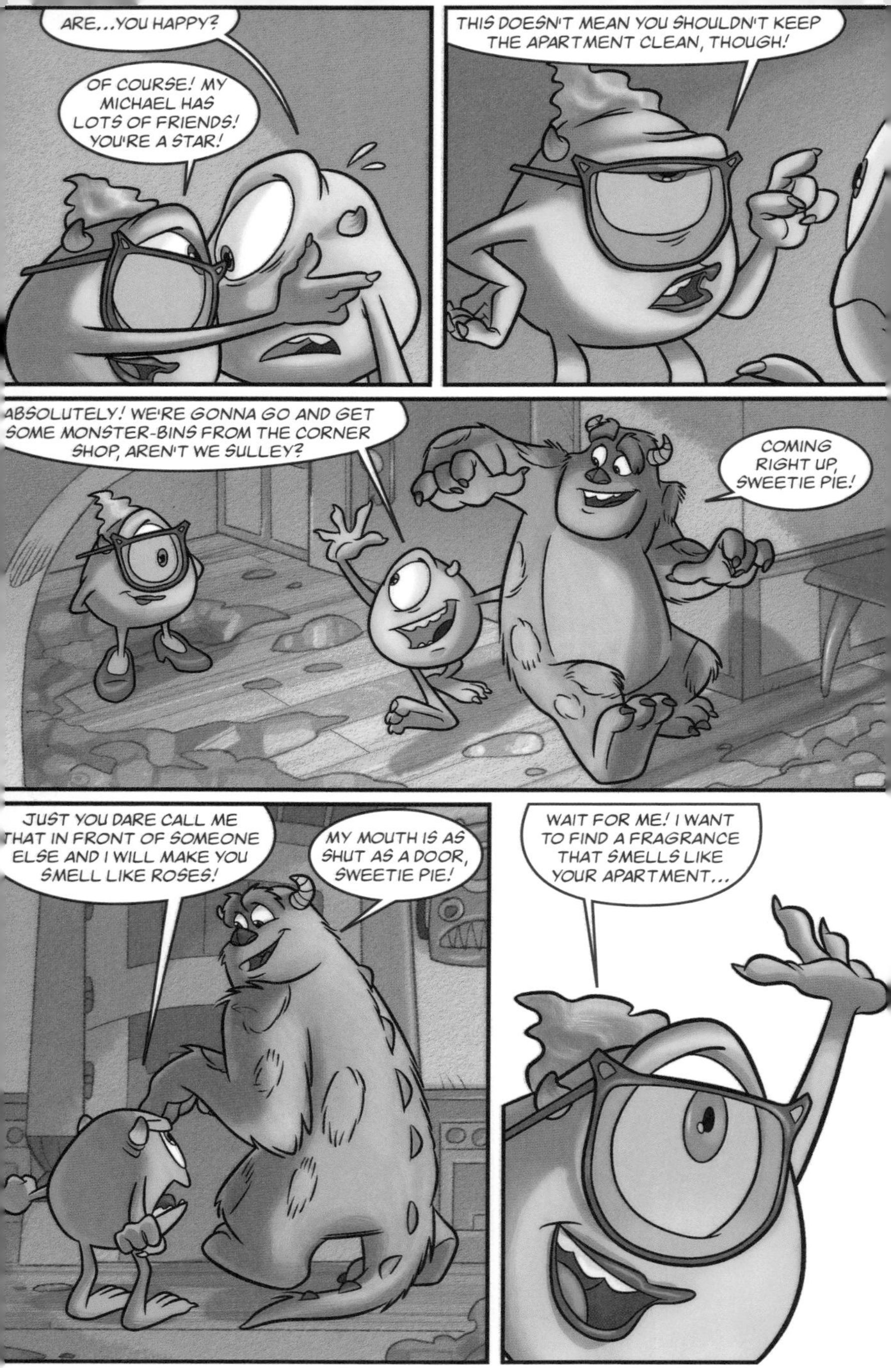
ARE...YOU HAPPY?
OF COURSE! MY MICHAEL HAS LOTS OF FRIENDS! YOU'RE A STAR!
THIS DOESN'T MEAN YOU SHOULDN'T KEEP THE APARTMENT CLEAN, THOUGH!
ABSOLUTELY! WE'RE GONNA GO AND GET SOME MONSTER-BINS FROM THE CORNER SHOP, AREN'T WE SULLEY?
COMING RIGHT UP, SWEETIE PIE!
JUST YOU DARE CALL ME THAT IN FRONT OF SOMEONE ELSE AND I WILL MAKE YOU SMELL LIKE ROSES!
MY MOUTH IS AS SHUT AS A DOOR, SWEETIE PIE!
WAIT FOR ME! I WANT TO FIND A FRAGRANCE THAT SMELLS LIKE YOUR APARTMENT...

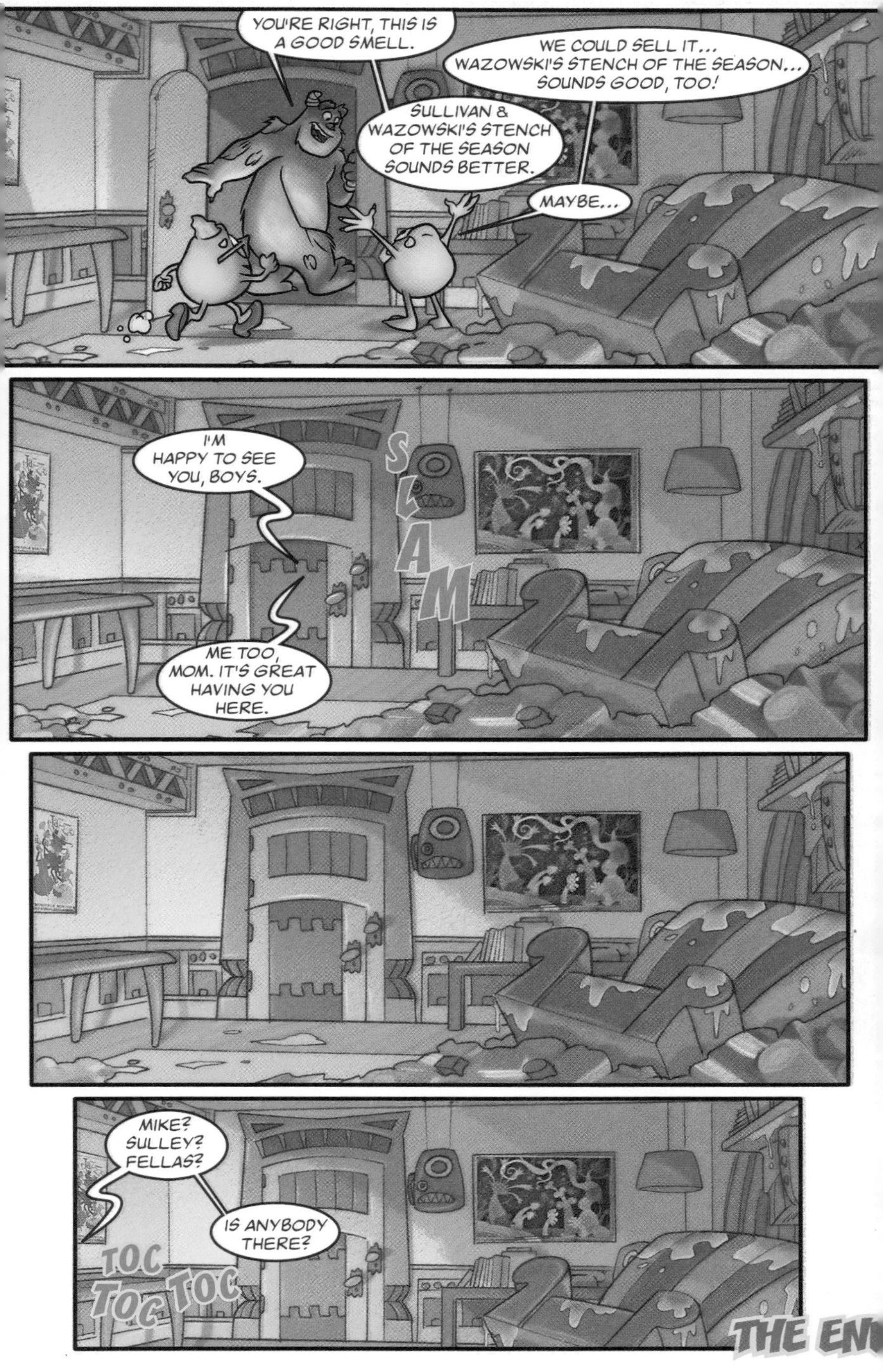

YOU'RE RIGHT, THIS IS A GOOD SMELL.
WE COULD SELL IT... WAZOWSKI'S STENCH OF THE SEASON... SOUNDS GOOD, TOO!
SULLIVAN & WAZOWSKI'S STENCH OF THE SEASON SOUNDS BETTER.
MAYBE...
I'M HAPPY TO SEE YOU, BOYS.
SLAM
ME TOO, MOM. IT'S GREAT HAVING YOU HERE.
MIKE? SULLEY? FELLAS?
IS ANYBODY THERE?
TOC TOC TOC
THE EN

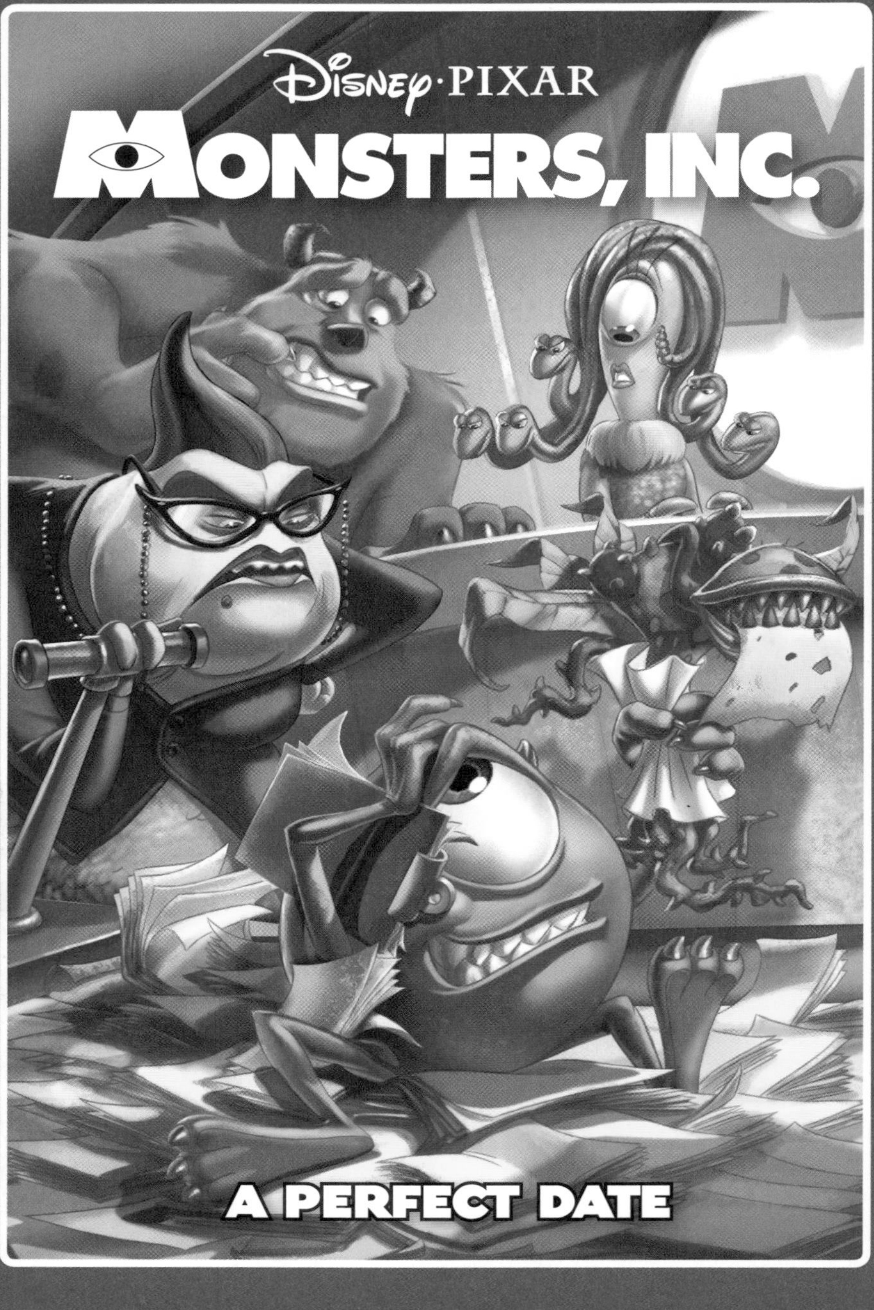
DISNEY·PIXAR
MONSTERS, INC.
A PERFECT DATE

MONSTROPOLIS. THE MOST FAMOUS SCARERS IN THE CITY ARE HAVING A GAME NIGHT AT MIKE AND SULLEY'S...

HEY! WAIT A SECOND...

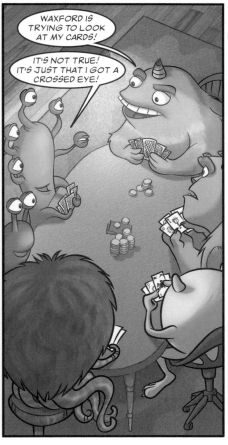

WAXFORD IS TRYING TO LOOK AT MY CARDS!

IT'S NOT TRUE! IT'S JUST THAT I GOT A CROSSED EYE!

C'MON GUYS, YOU'RE GROWN MONSTERS.

WHOSE TURN IS IT?

YOURS...

YOU'RE WASTING YOUR TIME, FELLAS. NO ONE CAN BEAT THE BEST PLAYER IN MONSTROPOLIS: MIKE WAZOWSK--

I'VE WON

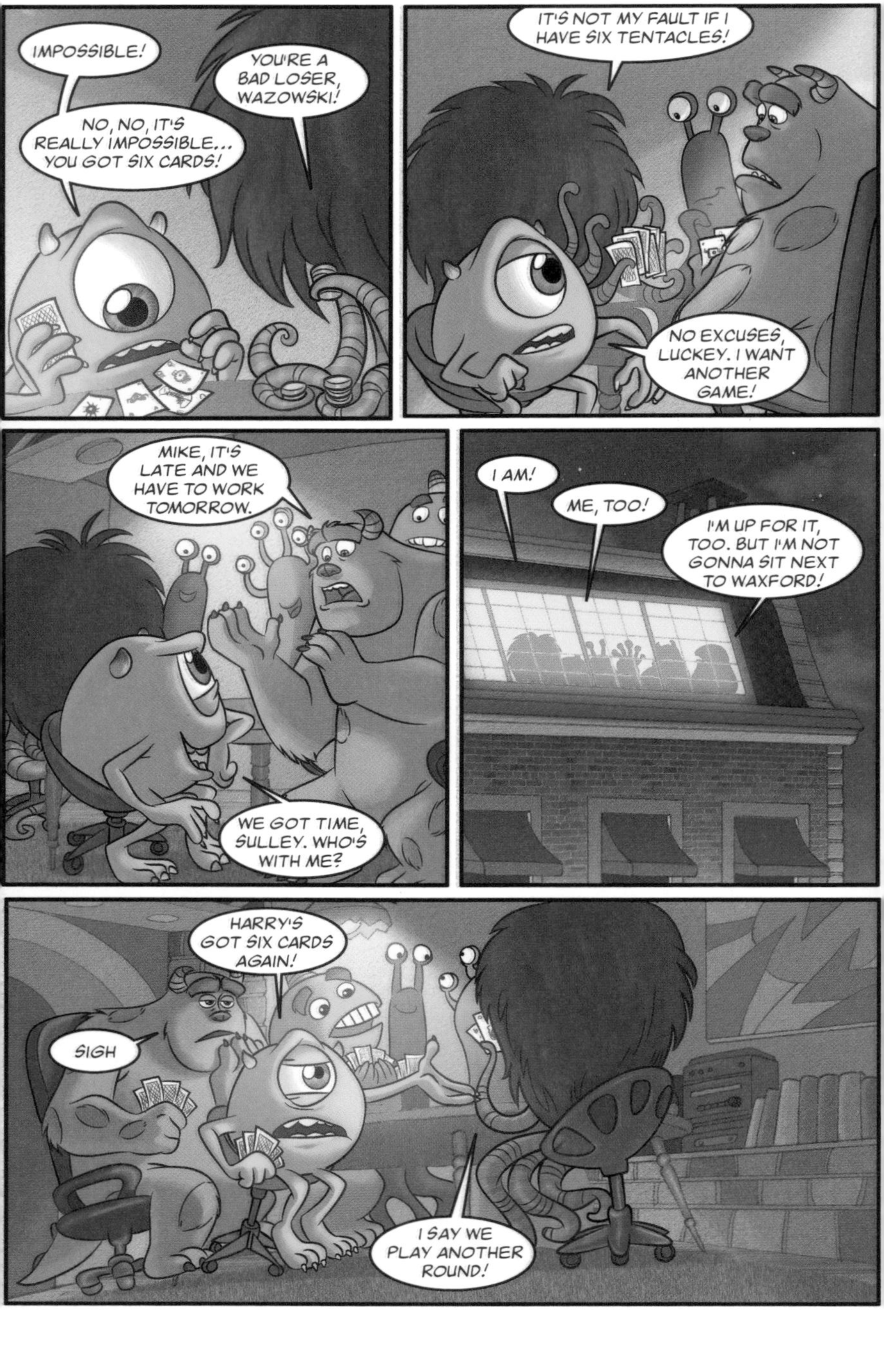
IMPOSSIBLE!
NO, NO, IT'S REALLY IMPOSSIBLE... YOU GOT SIX CARDS!
YOU'RE A BAD LOSER, WAZOWSKI!
IT'S NOT MY FAULT IF I HAVE SIX TENTACLES!
NO EXCUSES, LUCKEY. I WANT ANOTHER GAME!
MIKE, IT'S LATE AND WE HAVE TO WORK TOMORROW.
WE GOT TIME, SULLEY. WHO'S WITH ME?
I AM!
ME, TOO!
I'M UP FOR IT, TOO. BUT I'M NOT GONNA SIT NEXT TO WAXFORD!
HARRY'S GOT SIX CARDS AGAIN!
SIGH
I SAY WE PLAY ANOTHER ROUND!

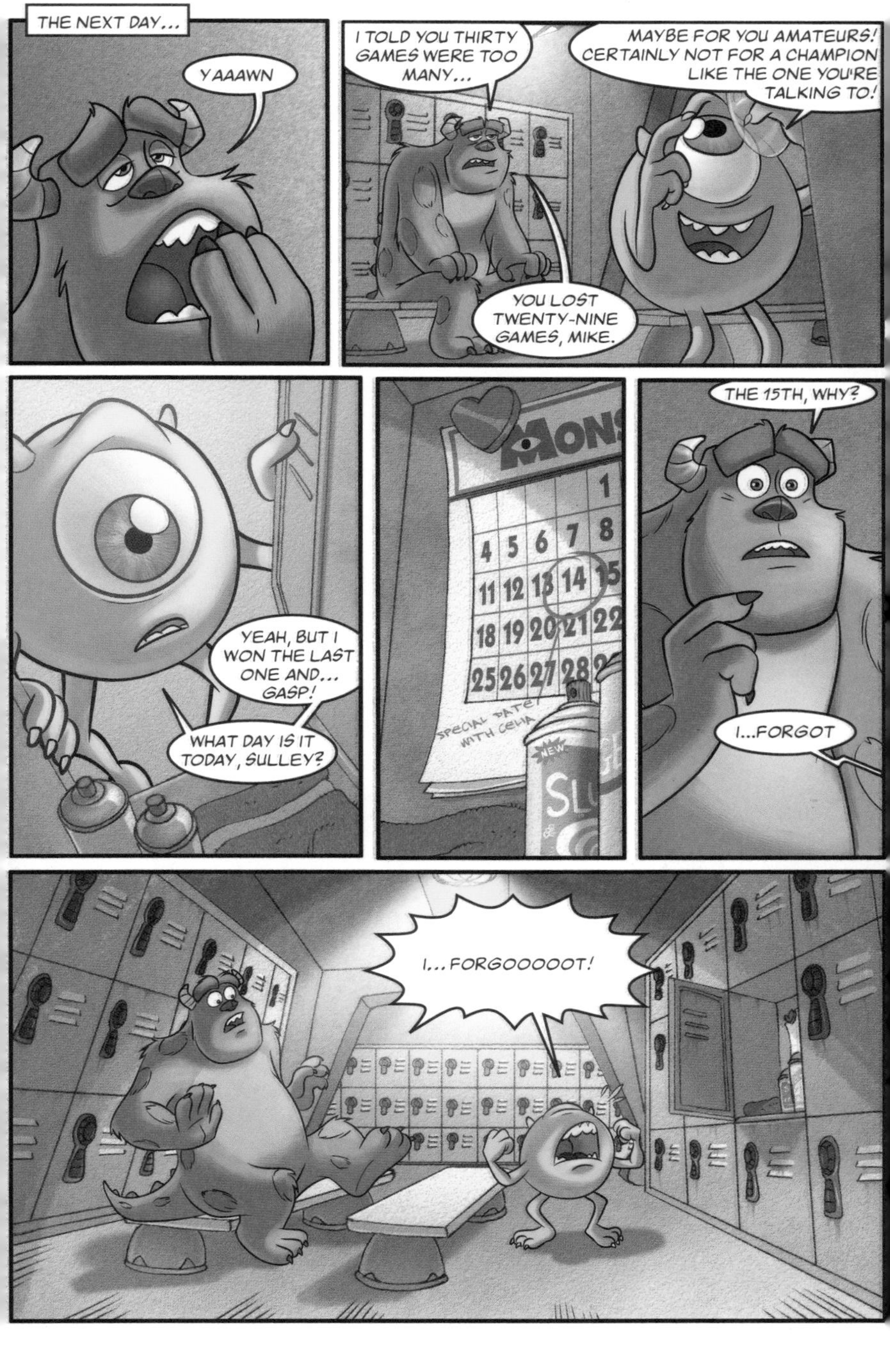
THE NEXT DAY...
YAAAWN
I TOLD YOU THIRTY GAMES WERE TOO MANY...
MAYBE FOR YOU AMATEURS! CERTAINLY NOT FOR A CHAMPION LIKE THE ONE YOU'RE TALKING TO!
YOU LOST TWENTY-NINE GAMES, MIKE.
YEAH, BUT I WON THE LAST ONE AND... GASP!
WHAT DAY IS IT TODAY, SULLEY?
SPECIAL DATE WITH CELIA
THE 15TH, WHY?
I...FORGOT
I... FORGOOOOOT!

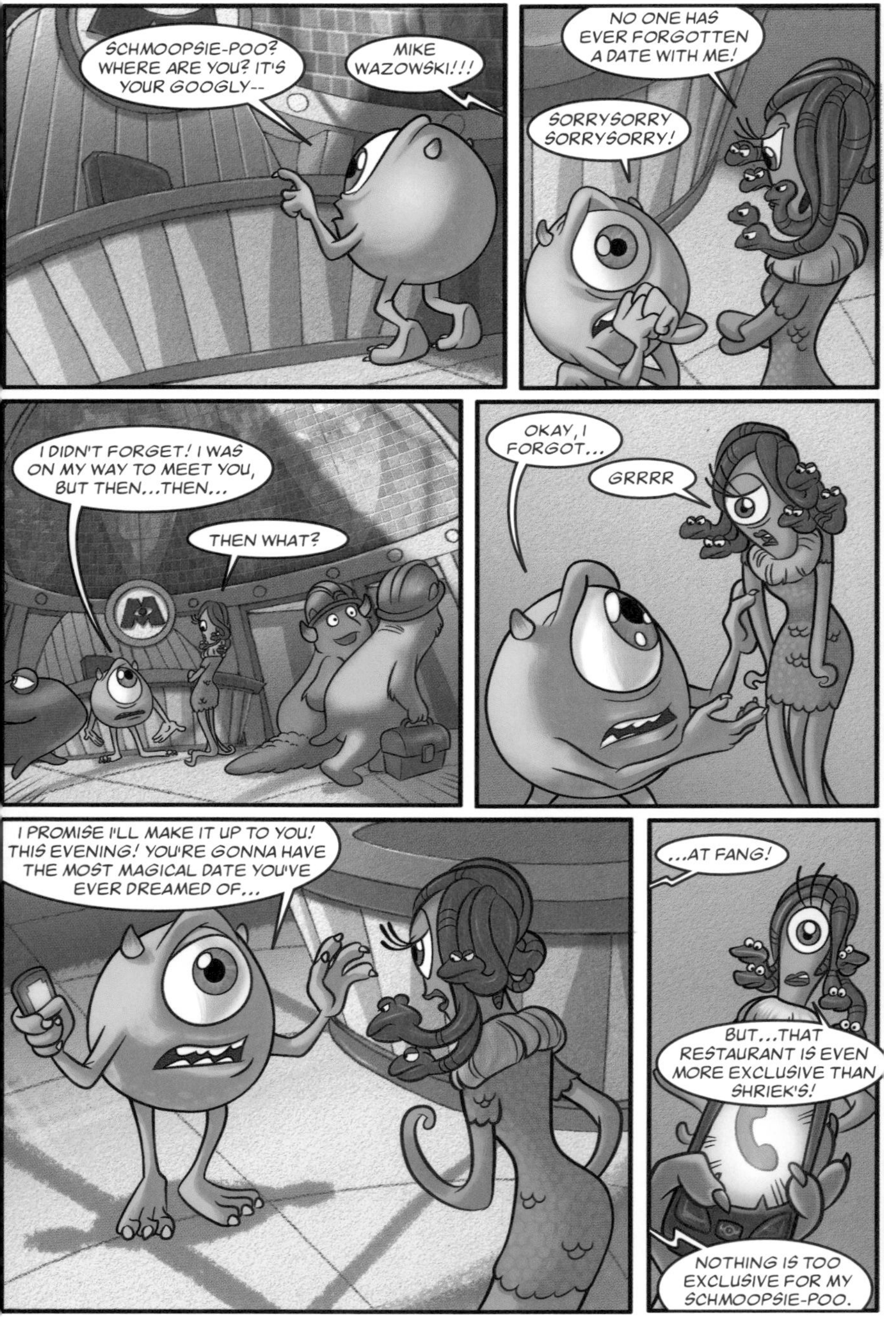
SCHMOOPSIE-POO? WHERE ARE YOU? IT'S YOUR GOOGLY--
MIKE WAZOWSKI!!!
NO ONE HAS EVER FORGOTTEN A DATE WITH ME!
SORRYSORRY SORRYSORRY!
I DIDN'T FORGET! I WAS ON MY WAY TO MEET YOU, BUT THEN...THEN...
THEN WHAT?
OKAY, I FORGOT...
GRRRR
I PROMISE I'LL MAKE IT UP TO YOU! THIS EVENING! YOU'RE GONNA HAVE THE MOST MAGICAL DATE YOU'VE EVER DREAMED OF...
...AT FANG!
BUT...THAT RESTAURANT IS EVEN MORE EXCLUSIVE THAN SHRIEK'S!
NOTHING IS TOO EXCLUSIVE FOR MY SCHMOOPSIE-POO.

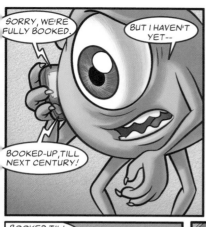

SORRY, WE'RE FULLY BOOKED.

BUT I HAVEN'T YET--

BOOKED-UP, TILL NEXT CENTURY!

HOW ABOUT A NICE EVENING AT SHRIEK'S?

TAPTAPTAP

BOOKED, TILL NEXT YEAR!

!

WHAT ABOUT... A PICNIC? A SUPER-ROMANTIC MOONLIT NIGHT?

MIKE, IF YOU LET ME DOWN AGAIN THIS EVENING, I...

WAZOWSKI!

ROZ?!

GUESS WHAT I HAVE.

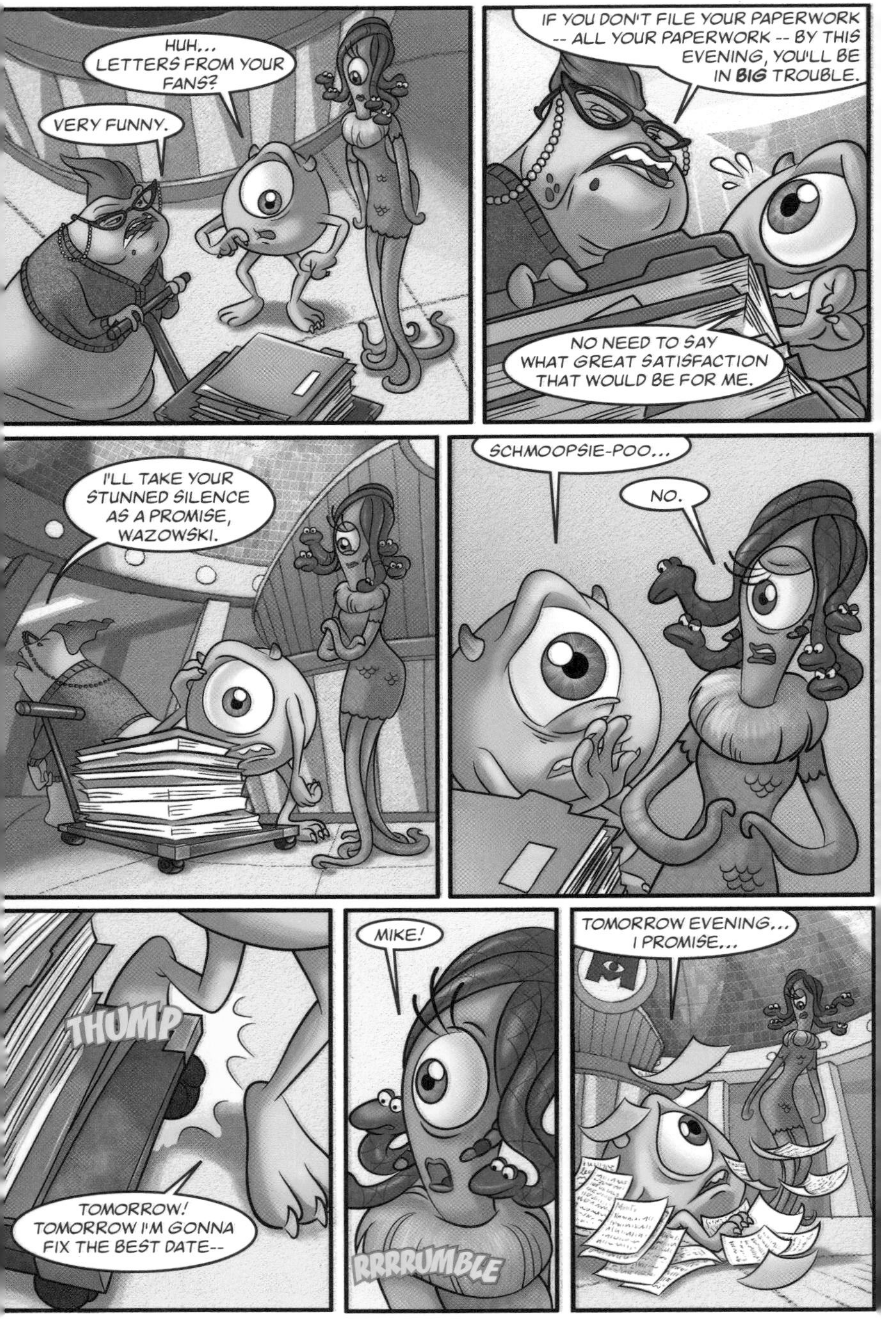
HUH... LETTERS FROM YOUR FANS?
VERY FUNNY.
IF YOU DON'T FILE YOUR PAPERWORK -- ALL YOUR PAPERWORK -- BY THIS EVENING, YOU'LL BE IN BIG TROUBLE.
NO NEED TO SAY WHAT GREAT SATISFACTION THAT WOULD BE FOR ME.
I'LL TAKE YOUR STUNNED SILENCE AS A PROMISE, WAZOWSKI.
SCHMOOPSIE-POO...
NO.
THUMP
TOMORROW! TOMORROW I'M GONNA FIX THE BEST DATE--
MIKE!
RRRRUMBLE
TOMORROW EVENING... I PROMISE...

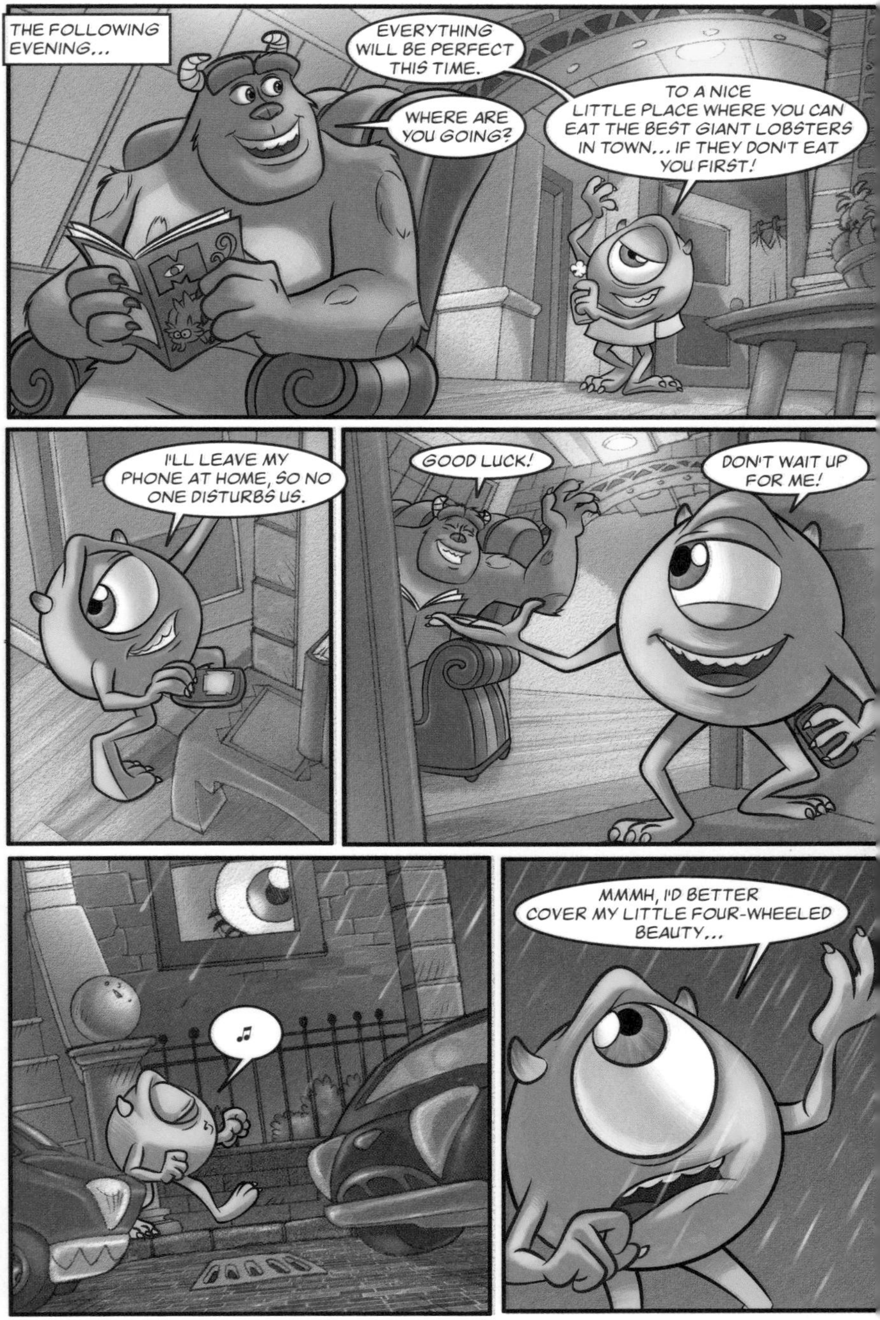
THE FOLLOWING EVENING...
WHERE ARE YOU GOING?
EVERYTHING WILL BE PERFECT THIS TIME.
TO A NICE LITTLE PLACE WHERE YOU CAN EAT THE BEST GIANT LOBSTERS IN TOWN... IF THEY DON'T EAT YOU FIRST!
I'LL LEAVE MY PHONE AT HOME, SO NO ONE DISTURBS US.
GOOD LUCK!
DON'T WAIT UP FOR ME!
♫
MMMH, I'D BETTER COVER MY LITTLE FOUR-WHEELED BEAUTY...

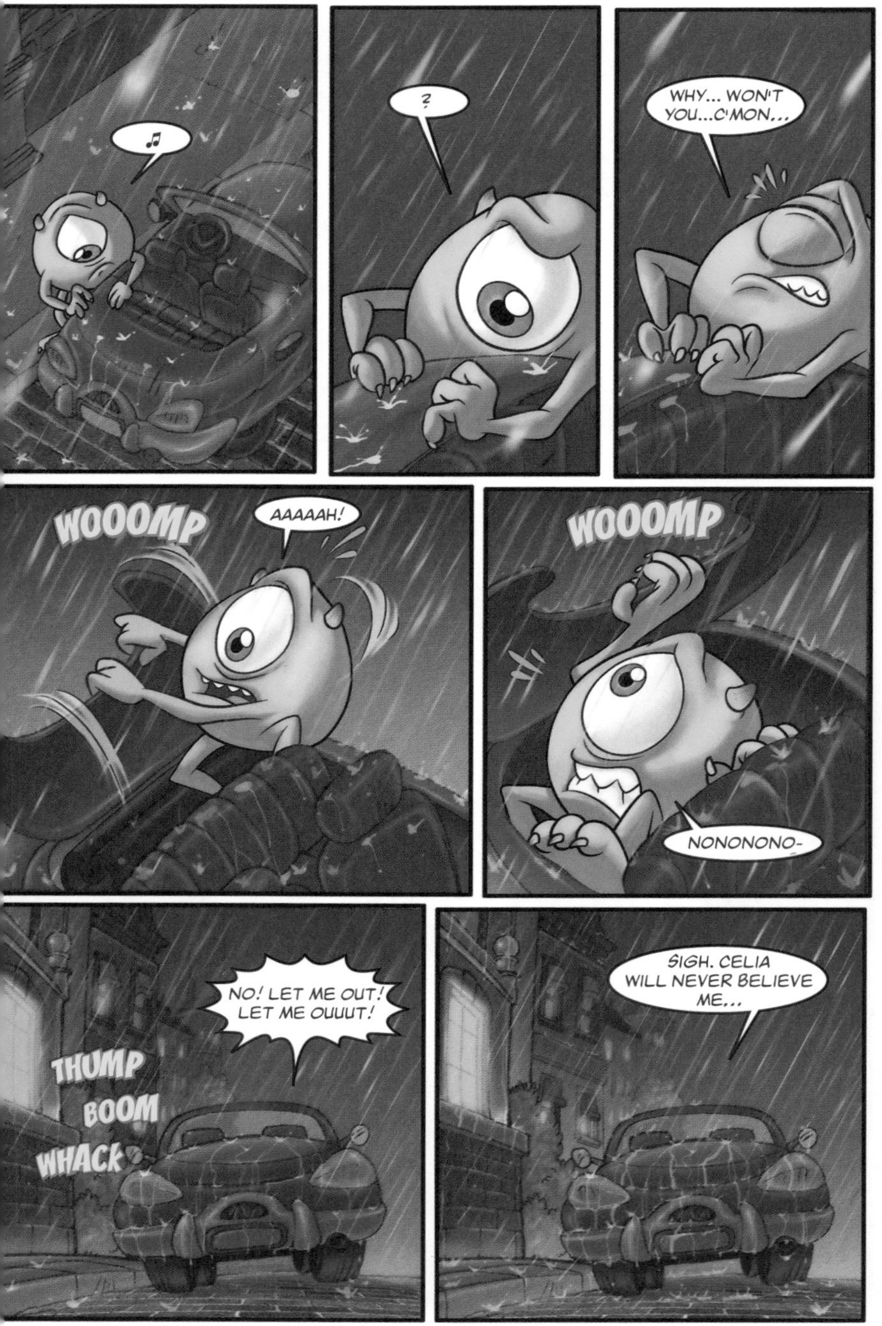
♪
?
WHY... WON'T YOU...C'MON...
WOOOMP
AAAAAH!
WOOOMP
NONONONO-
NO! LET ME OUT! LET ME OUUUT!
THUMP
BOOM
WHACK
SIGH. CELIA WILL NEVER BELIEVE ME...

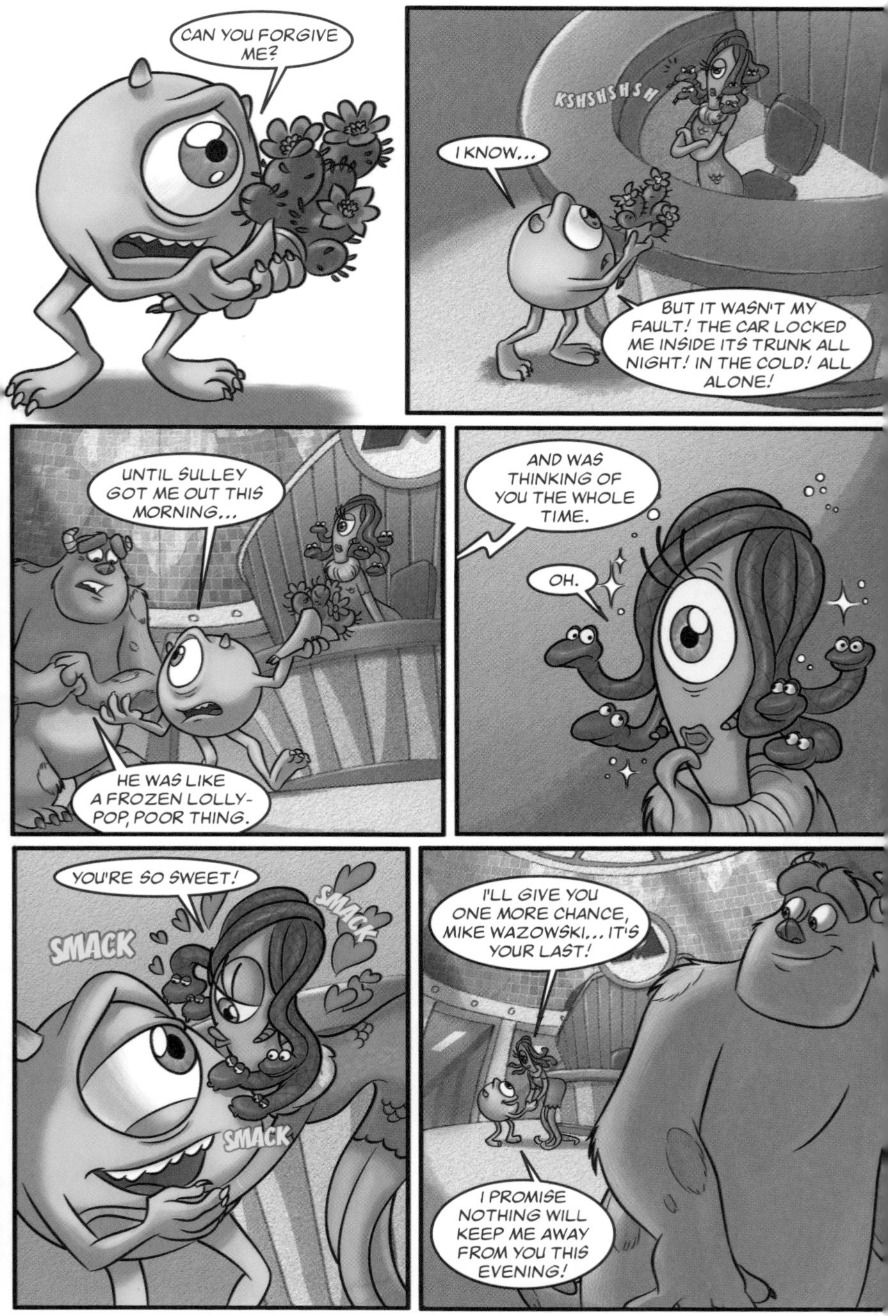
CAN YOU FORGIVE ME?
KSHSHSHSH
I KNOW...
BUT IT WASN'T MY FAULT! THE CAR LOCKED ME INSIDE ITS TRUNK ALL NIGHT! IN THE COLD! ALL ALONE!
UNTIL SULLEY GOT ME OUT THIS MORNING...
HE WAS LIKE A FROZEN LOLLY-POP, POOR THING.
AND WAS THINKING OF YOU THE WHOLE TIME.
OH.
YOU'RE SO SWEET!
SMACK
SMACK
SMACK
I'LL GIVE YOU ONE MORE CHANCE, MIKE WAZOWSKI... IT'S YOUR LAST!
I PROMISE NOTHING WILL KEEP ME AWAY FROM YOU THIS EVENING!

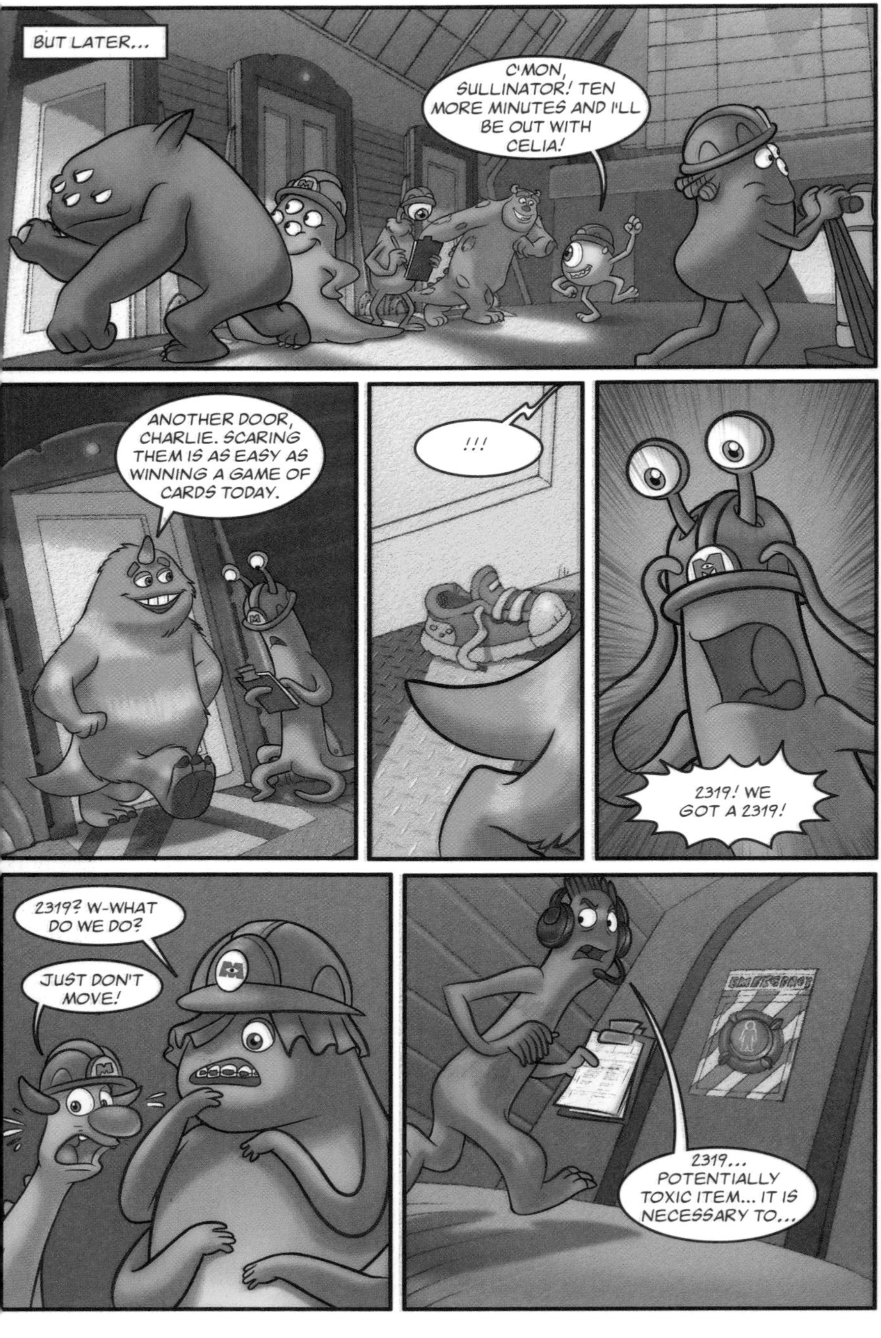
BUT LATER...
C'MON, SULLINATOR! TEN MORE MINUTES AND I'LL BE OUT WITH CELIA!
ANOTHER DOOR, CHARLIE. SCARING THEM IS AS EASY AS WINNING A GAME OF CARDS TODAY.
!!!
2319! WE GOT A 2319!
2319? W-WHAT DO WE DO?
JUST DON'T MOVE!
2319... POTENTIALLY TOXIC ITEM... IT IS NECESSARY TO...

WEEEOOOOO

...ISOLATION! ISOLATION SCARE FLOOR F.!

NO!

CLANK

WRRRRRRRR

NO! NO! NO!

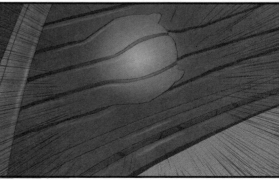

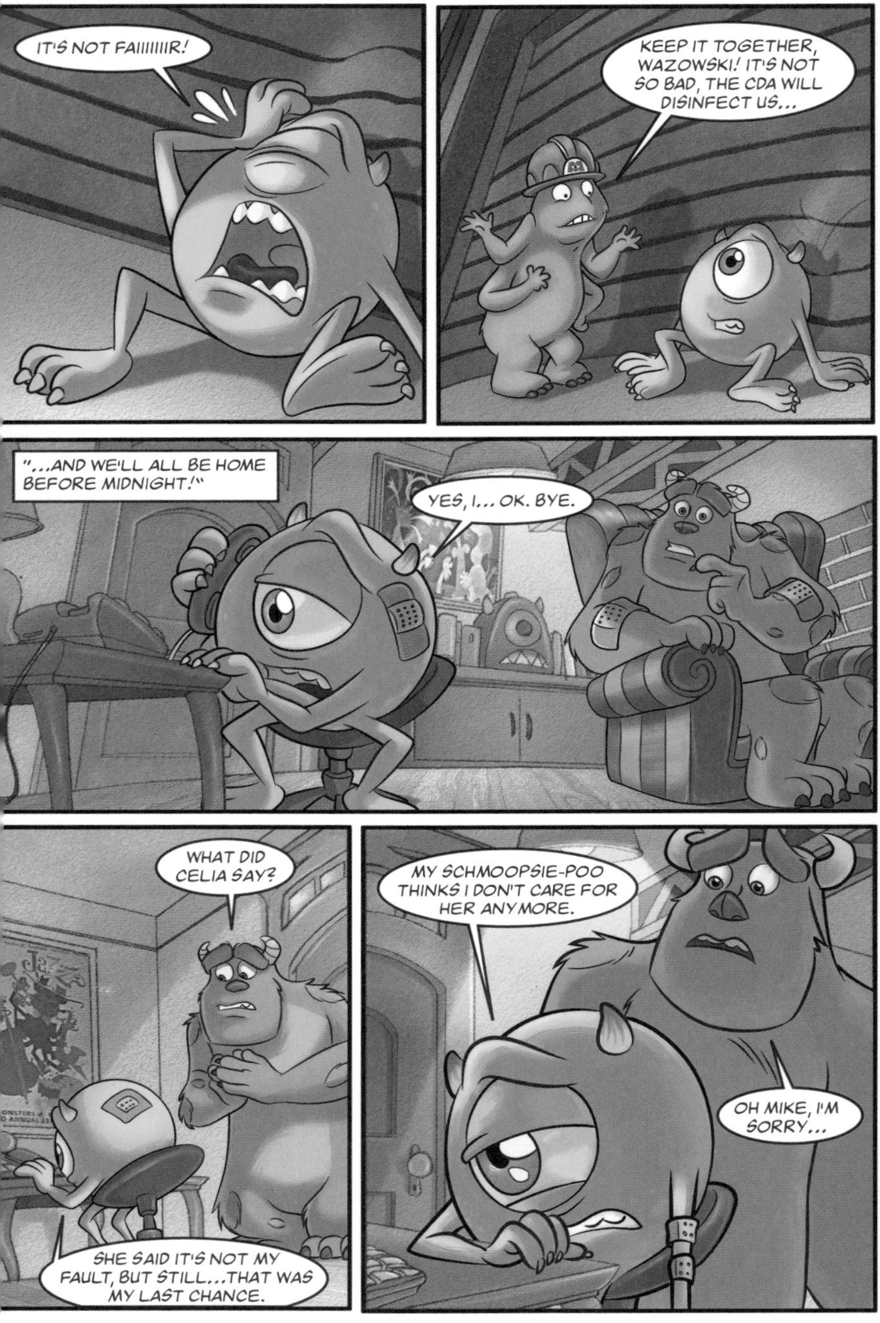
IT'S NOT FAIIIIIIIR!
KEEP IT TOGETHER, WAZOWSKI! IT'S NOT SO BAD, THE CDA WILL DISINFECT US...
"...AND WE'LL ALL BE HOME BEFORE MIDNIGHT!"
YES, I... OK. BYE.
WHAT DID CELIA SAY?
SHE SAID IT'S NOT MY FAULT, BUT STILL...THAT WAS MY LAST CHANCE.
MY SCHMOOPSIE-POO THINKS I DON'T CARE FOR HER ANYMORE.
OH MIKE, I'M SORRY...

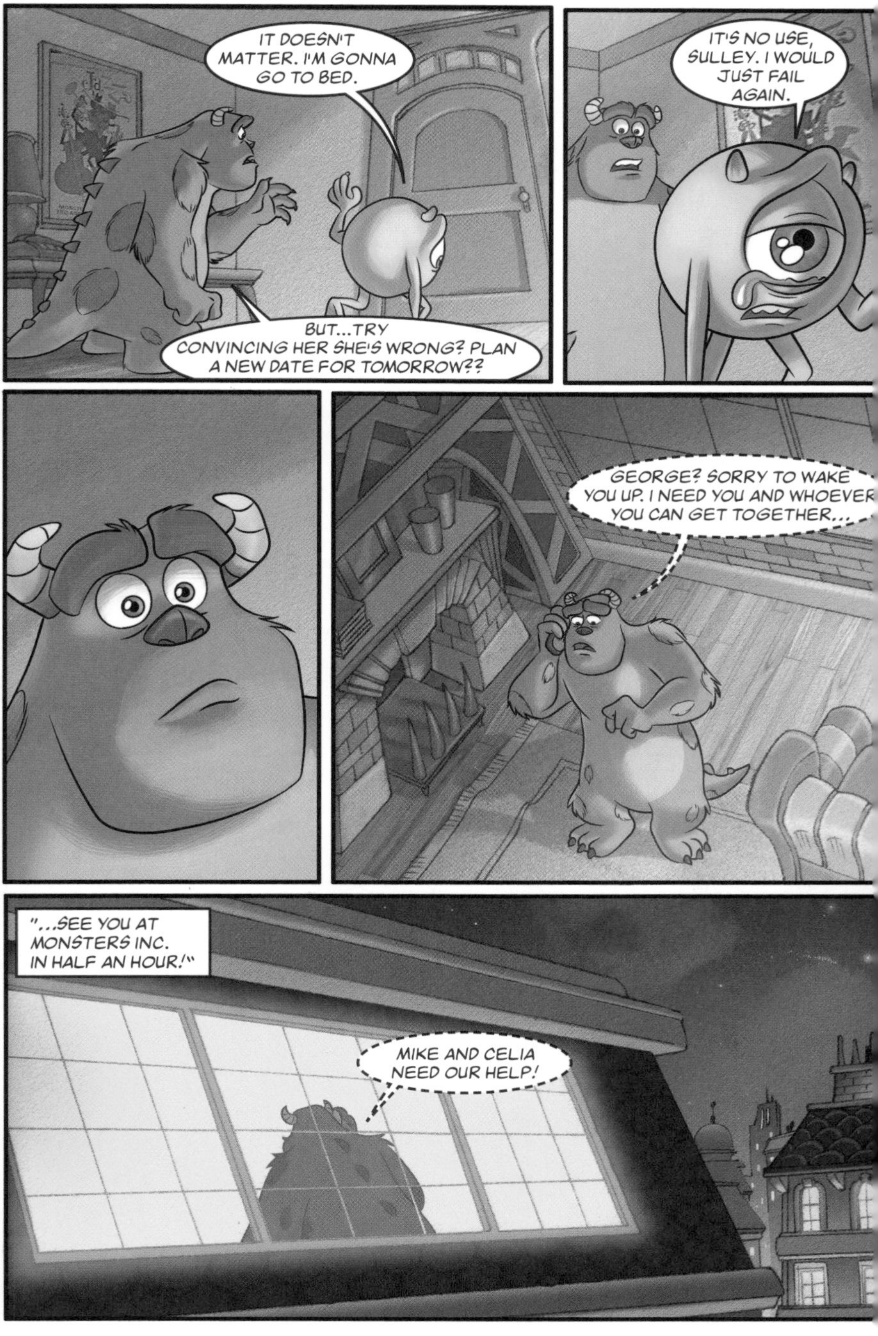
IT DOESN'T MATTER. I'M GONNA GO TO BED.
BUT...TRY CONVINCING HER SHE'S WRONG? PLAN A NEW DATE FOR TOMORROW??
IT'S NO USE, SULLEY. I WOULD JUST FAIL AGAIN.
GEORGE? SORRY TO WAKE YOU UP. I NEED YOU AND WHOEVER YOU CAN GET TOGETHER...
"...SEE YOU AT MONSTERS INC. IN HALF AN HOUR!"
MIKE AND CELIA NEED OUR HELP!

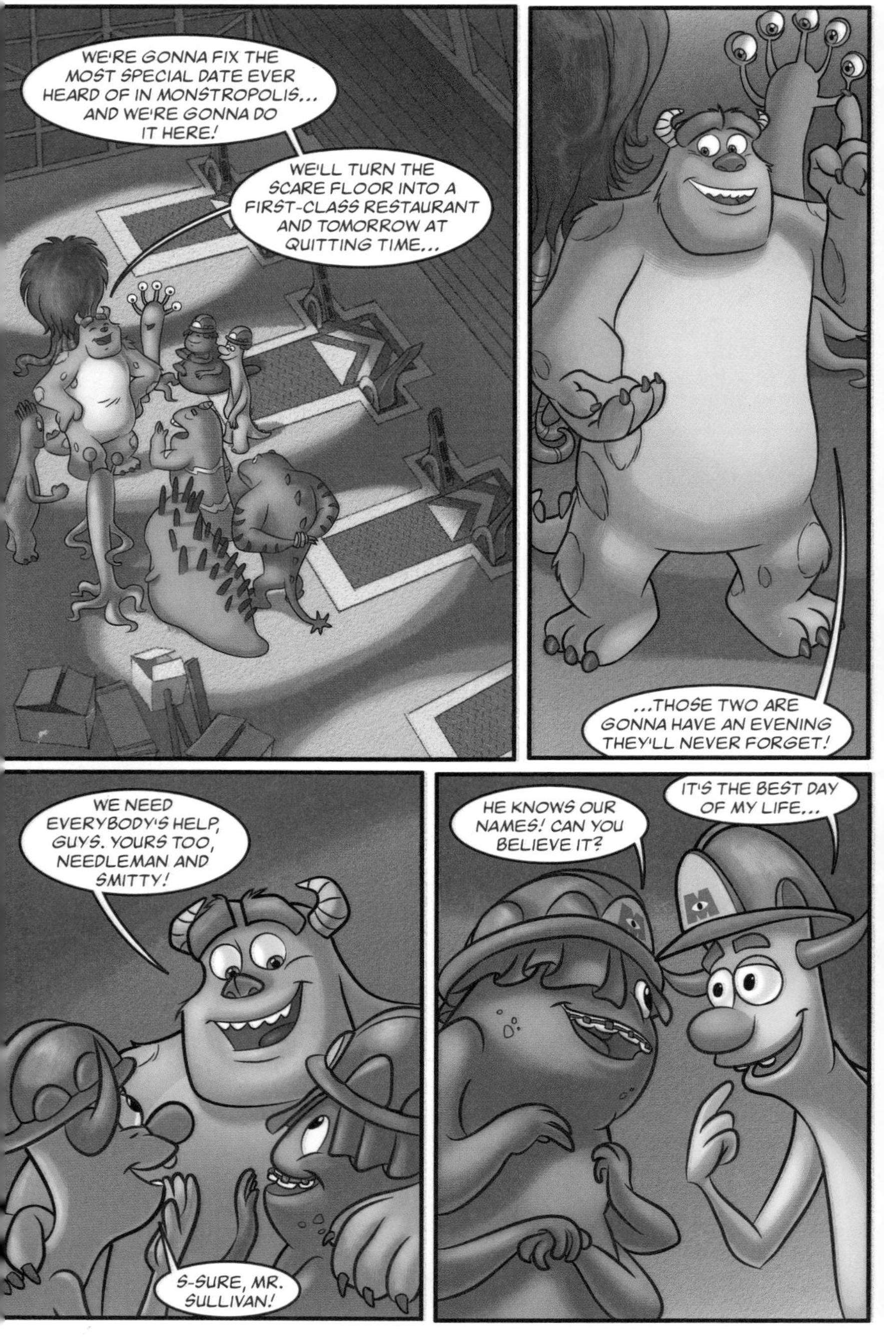
WE'RE GONNA FIX THE MOST SPECIAL DATE EVER HEARD OF IN MONSTROPOLIS... AND WE'RE GONNA DO IT HERE!
WE'LL TURN THE SCARE FLOOR INTO A FIRST-CLASS RESTAURANT AND TOMORROW AT QUITTING TIME...
...THOSE TWO ARE GONNA HAVE AN EVENING THEY'LL NEVER FORGET!
WE NEED EVERYBODY'S HELP, GUYS. YOURS TOO, NEEDLEMAN AND SMITTY!
S-SURE, MR. SULLIVAN!
HE KNOWS OUR NAMES! CAN YOU BELIEVE IT?
IT'S THE BEST DAY OF MY LIFE...

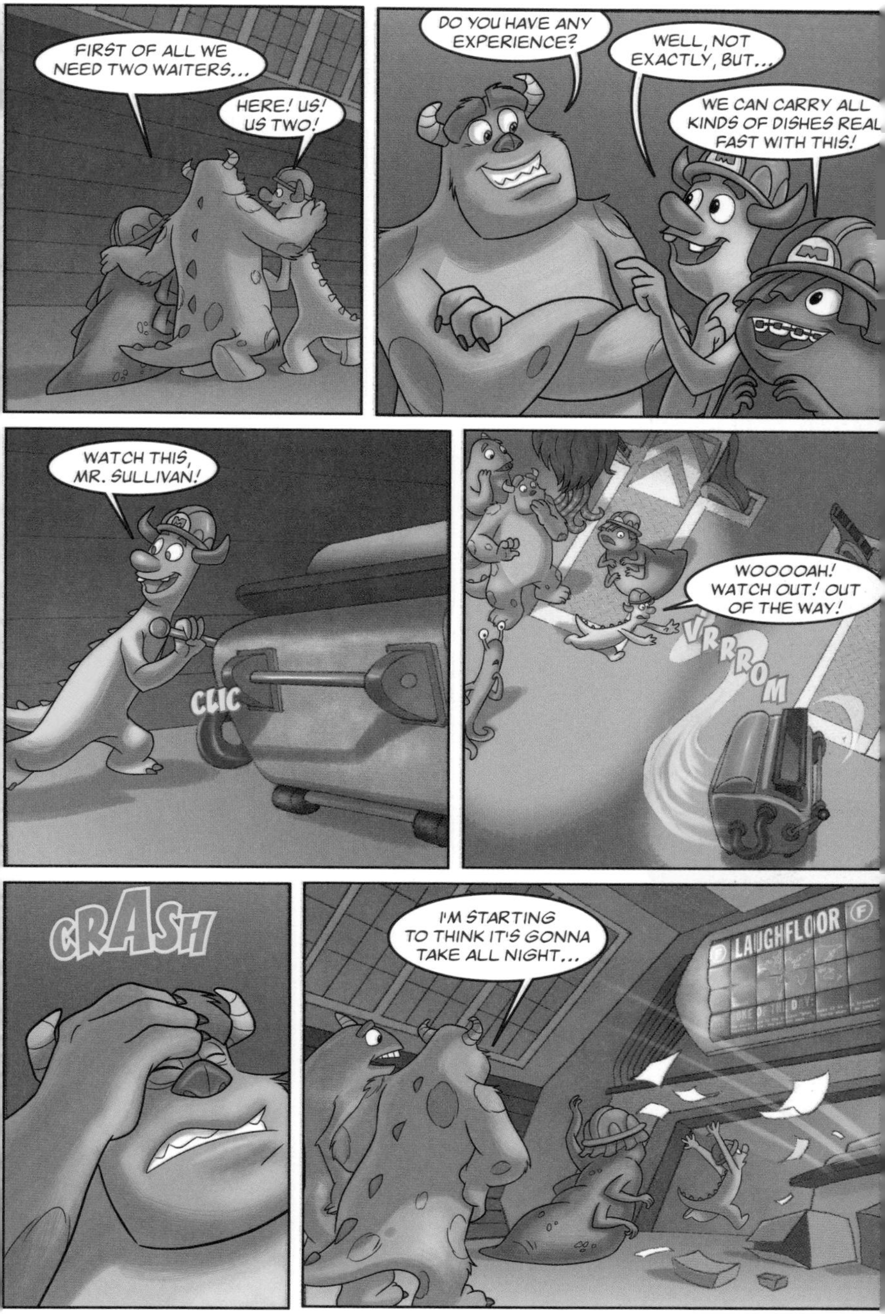
FIRST OF ALL WE NEED TWO WAITERS...
HERE! US! US TWO!
DO YOU HAVE ANY EXPERIENCE?
WELL, NOT EXACTLY, BUT...
WE CAN CARRY ALL KINDS OF DISHES REAL FAST WITH THIS!
WATCH THIS, MR. SULLIVAN!
CLIC
WOOOOAH! WATCH OUT! OUT OF THE WAY!
VRRROM
CRASH
I'M STARTING TO THINK IT'S GONNA TAKE ALL NIGHT...
LAUGHFLOOR

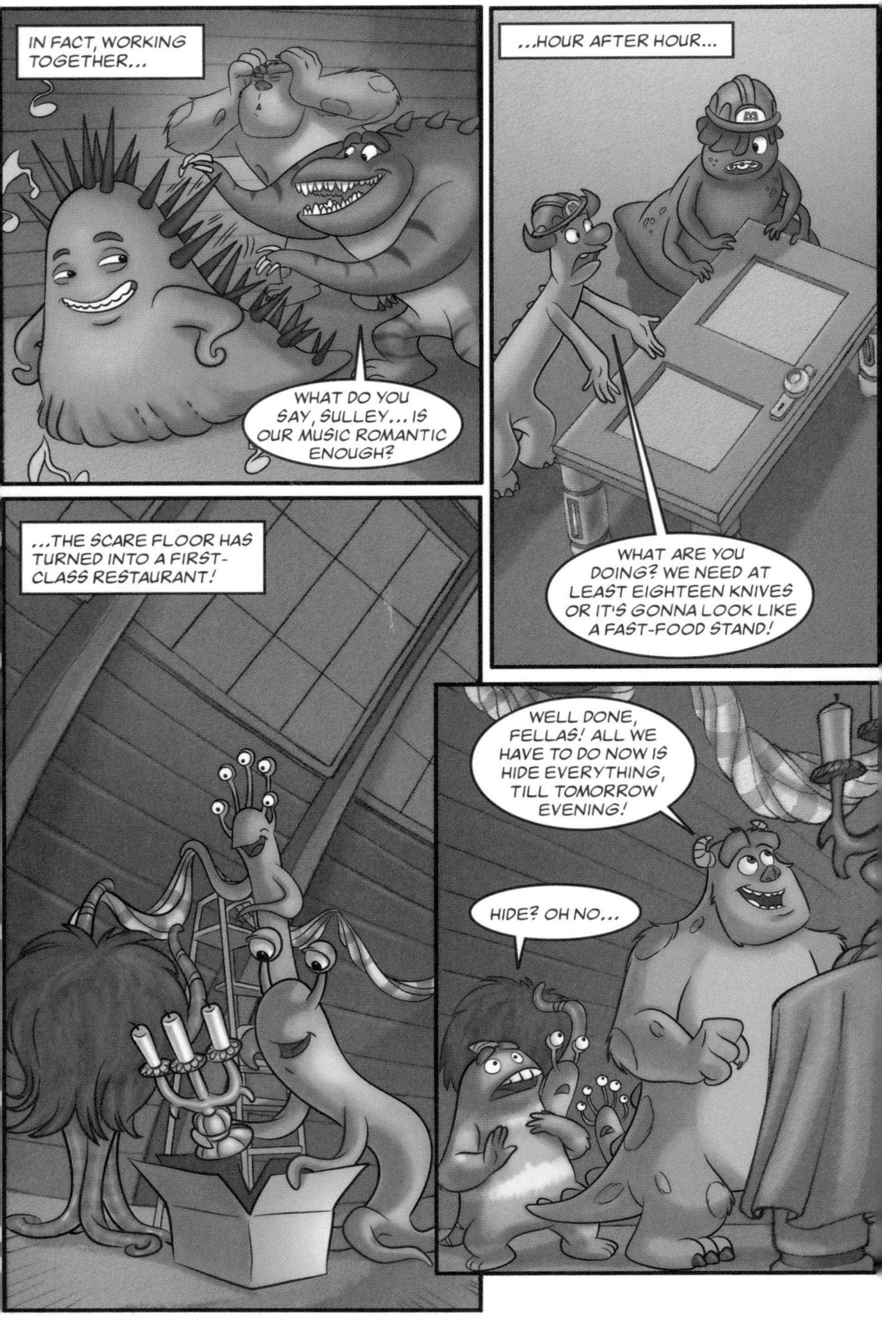
IN FACT, WORKING TOGETHER...
WHAT DO YOU SAY, SULLEY... IS OUR MUSIC ROMANTIC ENOUGH?
...HOUR AFTER HOUR...
WHAT ARE YOU DOING? WE NEED AT LEAST EIGHTEEN KNIVES OR IT'S GONNA LOOK LIKE A FAST-FOOD STAND!
...THE SCARE FLOOR HAS TURNED INTO A FIRST-CLASS RESTAURANT!
WELL DONE, FELLAS! ALL WE HAVE TO DO NOW IS HIDE EVERYTHING, TILL TOMORROW EVENING!
HIDE? OH NO...

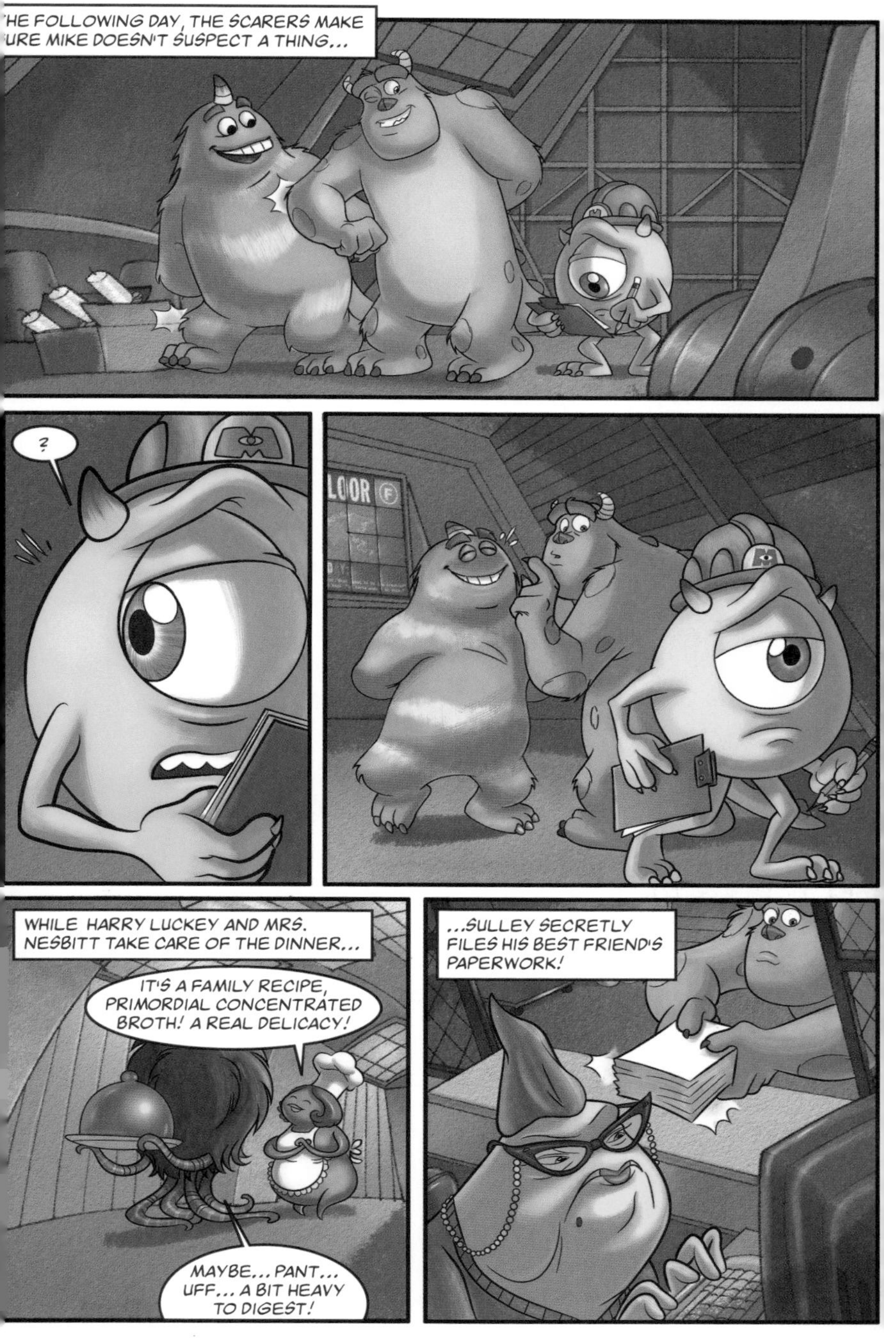
THE FOLLOWING DAY, THE SCARERS MAKE SURE MIKE DOESN'T SUSPECT A THING...
?
WHILE HARRY LUCKEY AND MRS. NESBITT TAKE CARE OF THE DINNER...
IT'S A FAMILY RECIPE, PRIMORDIAL CONCENTRATED BROTH! A REAL DELICACY!
MAYBE... PANT... UFF... A BIT HEAVY TO DIGEST!
...SULLEY SECRETLY FILES HIS BEST FRIEND'S PAPERWORK!

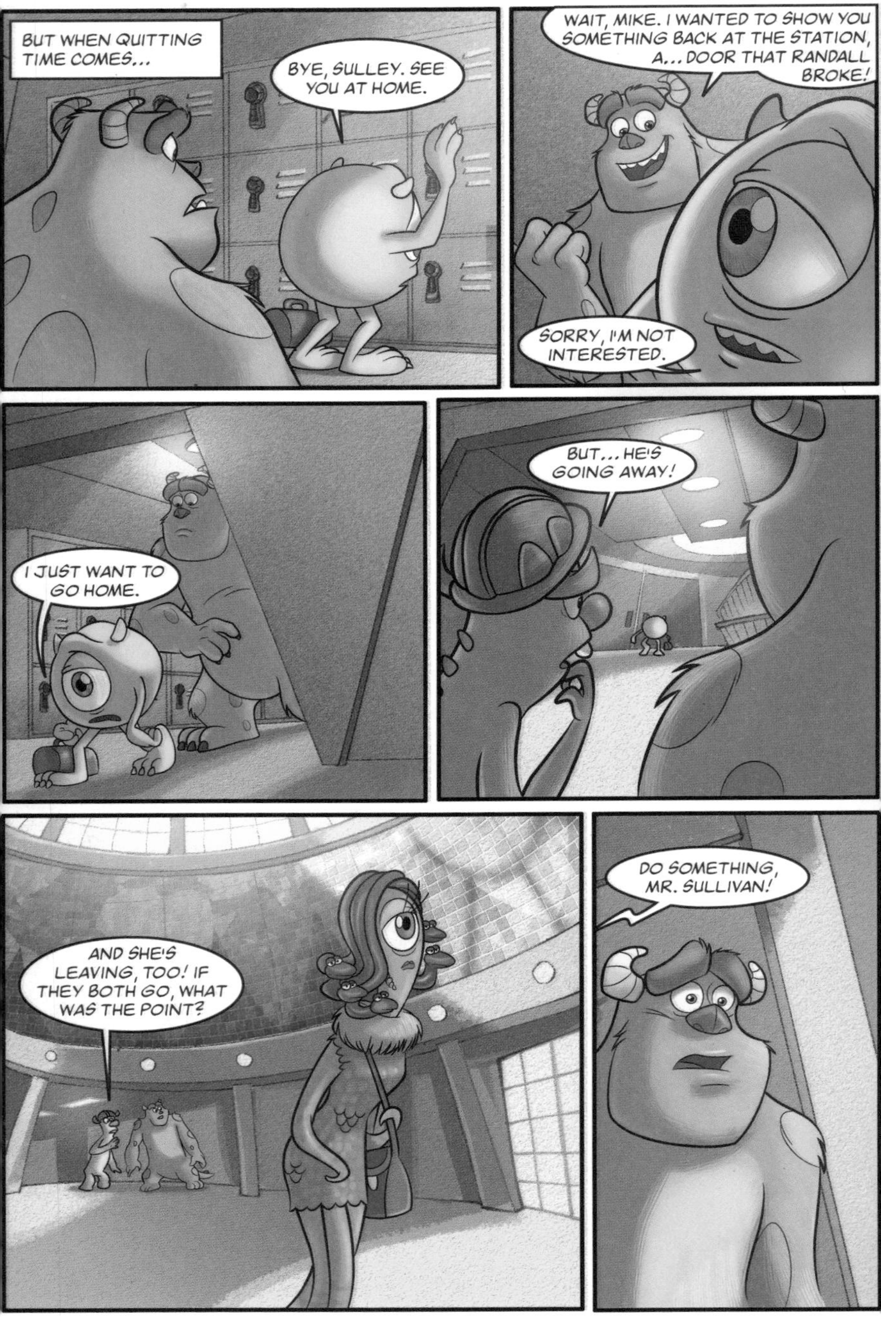
BUT WHEN QUITTING TIME COMES...
BYE, SULLEY. SEE YOU AT HOME.
WAIT, MIKE. I WANTED TO SHOW YOU SOMETHING BACK AT THE STATION, A... DOOR THAT RANDALL BROKE!
SORRY, I'M NOT INTERESTED.
I JUST WANT TO GO HOME.
BUT... HE'S GOING AWAY!
AND SHE'S LEAVING, TOO! IF THEY BOTH GO, WHAT WAS THE POINT?
DO SOMETHING, MR. SULLIVAN!

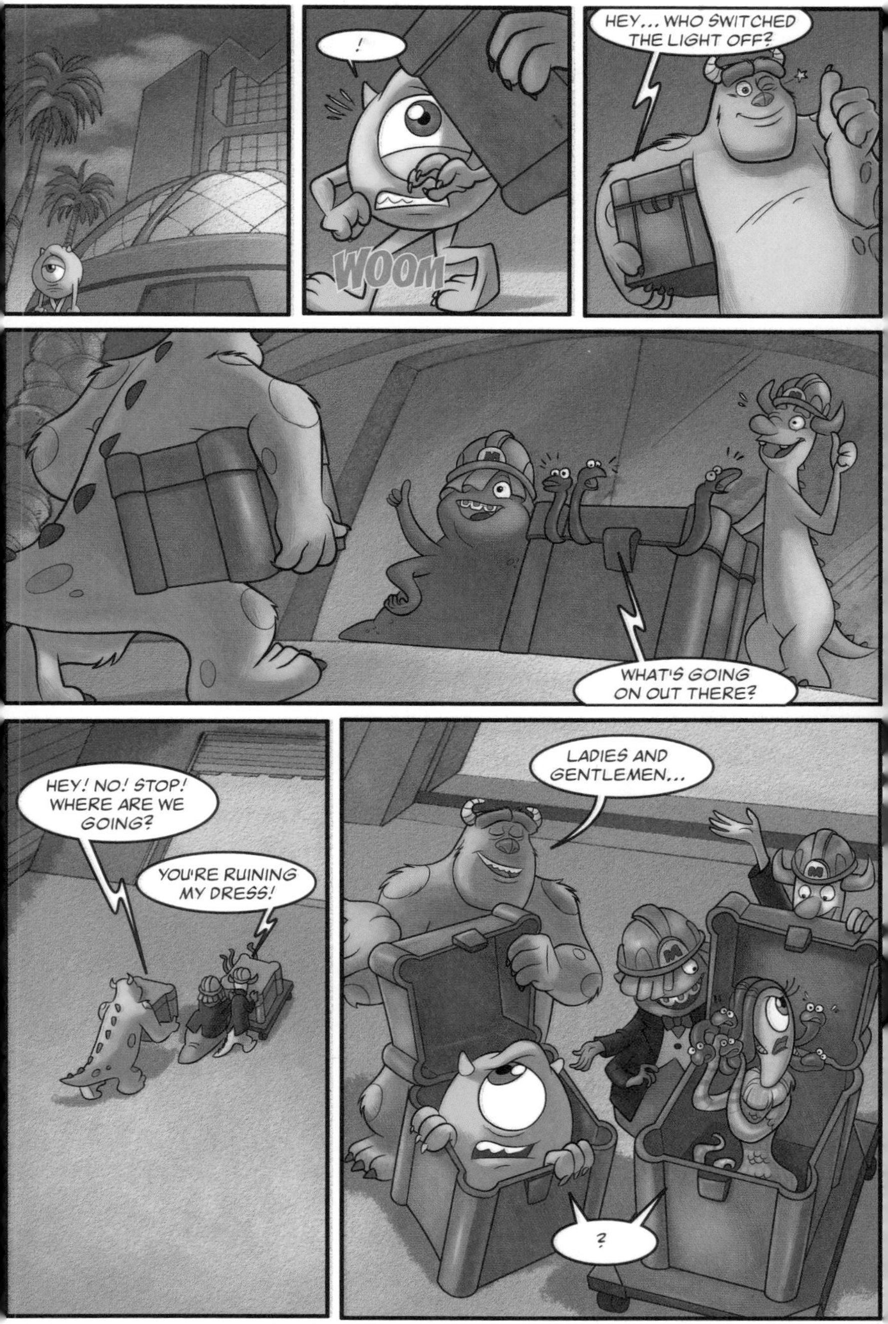
!
WOOM
HEY... WHO SWITCHED THE LIGHT OFF?
WHAT'S GOING ON OUT THERE?
HEY! NO! STOP! WHERE ARE WE GOING?
YOU'RE RUINING MY DRESS!
LADIES AND GENTLEMEN...
?

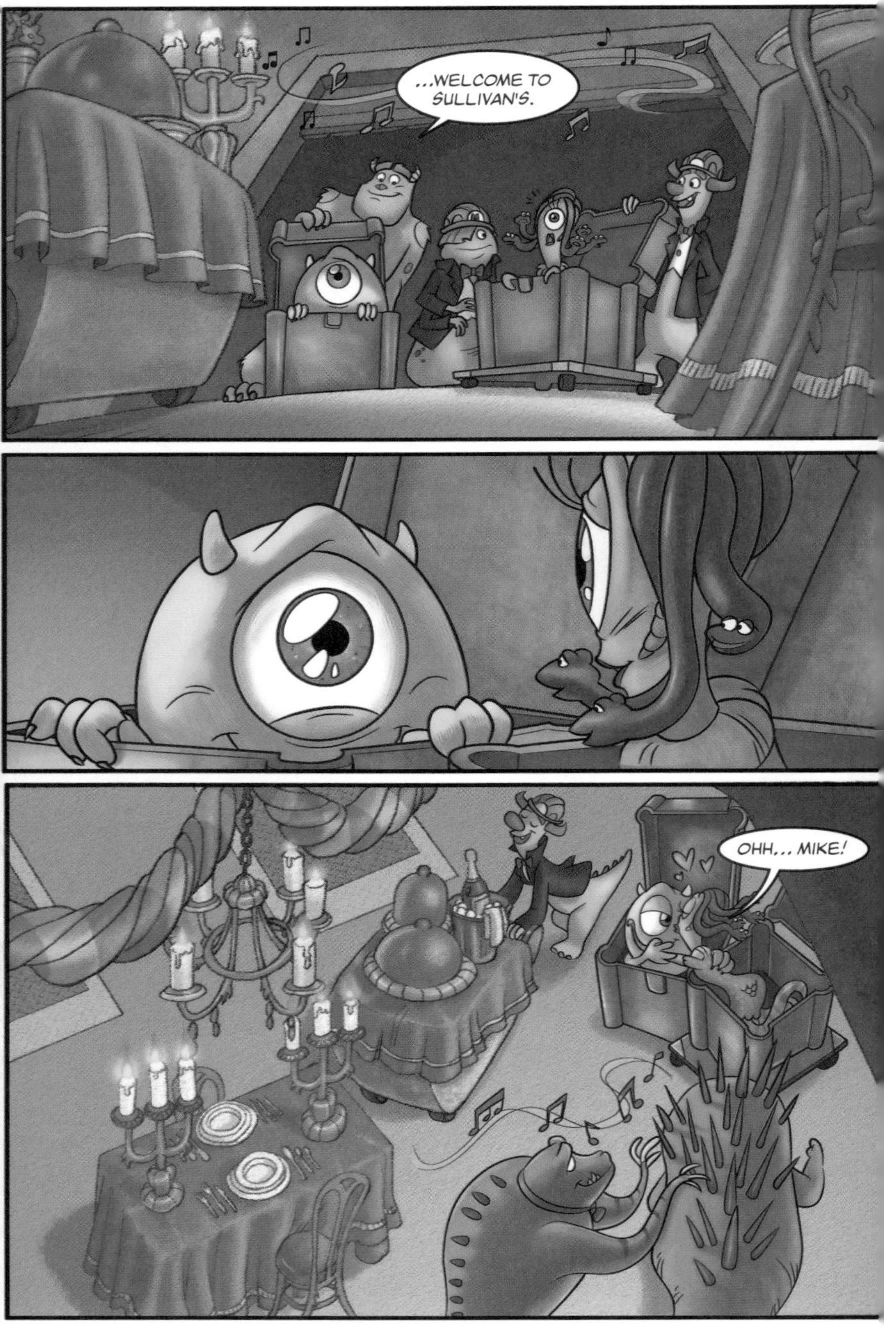
...WELCOME TO SULLIVAN'S.
OHH... MIKE!

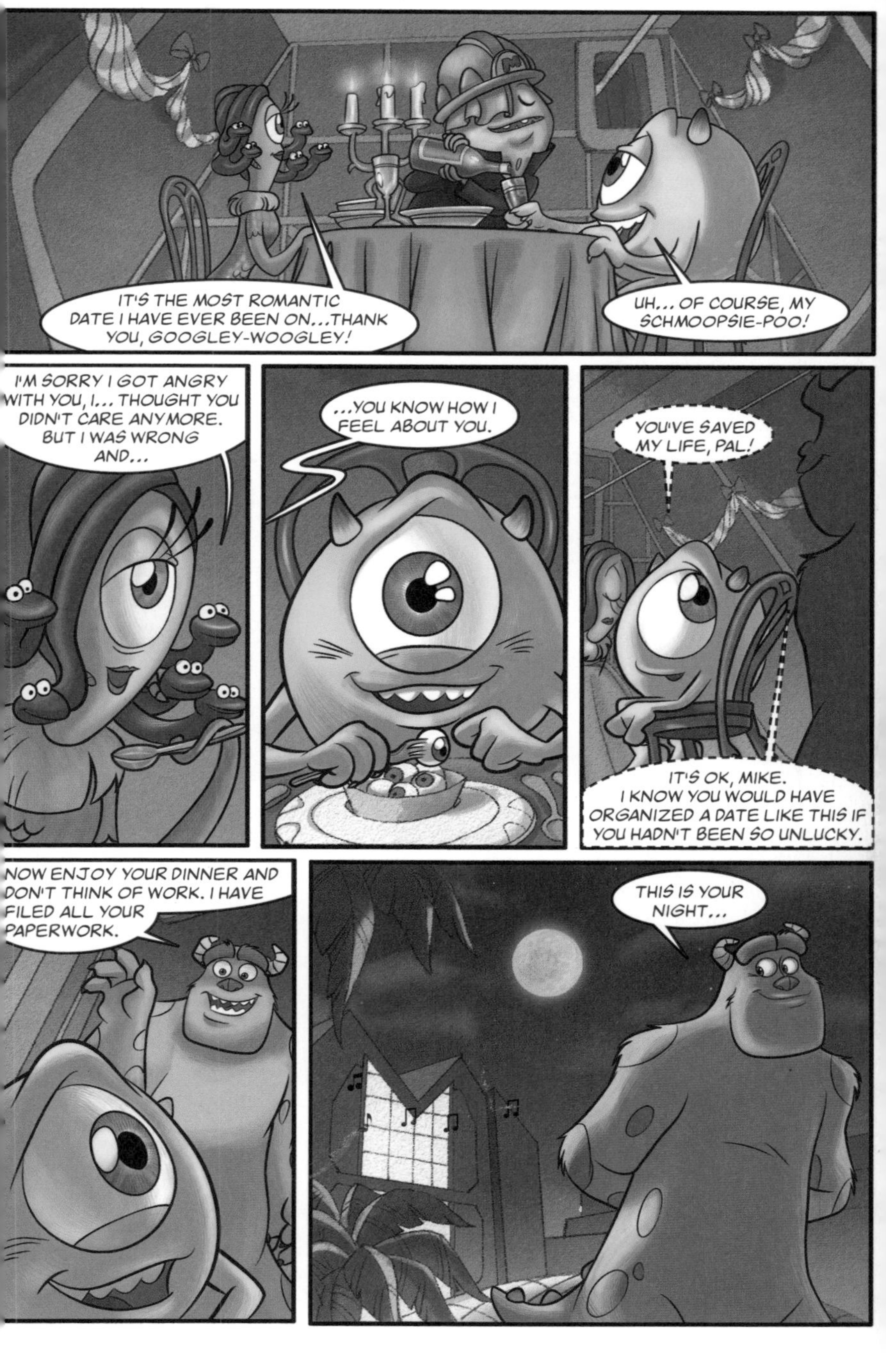
IT'S THE MOST ROMANTIC DATE I HAVE EVER BEEN ON...THANK YOU, GOOGLEY-WOOGLEY!
UH... OF COURSE, MY SCHMOOPSIE-POO!
I'M SORRY I GOT ANGRY WITH YOU, I... THOUGHT YOU DIDN'T CARE ANYMORE. BUT I WAS WRONG AND...
...YOU KNOW HOW I FEEL ABOUT YOU.
YOU'VE SAVED MY LIFE, PAL!
IT'S OK, MIKE. I KNOW YOU WOULD HAVE ORGANIZED A DATE LIKE THIS IF YOU HADN'T BEEN SO UNLUCKY.
NOW ENJOY YOUR DINNER AND DON'T THINK OF WORK. I HAVE FILED ALL YOUR PAPERWORK.
THIS IS YOUR NIGHT...

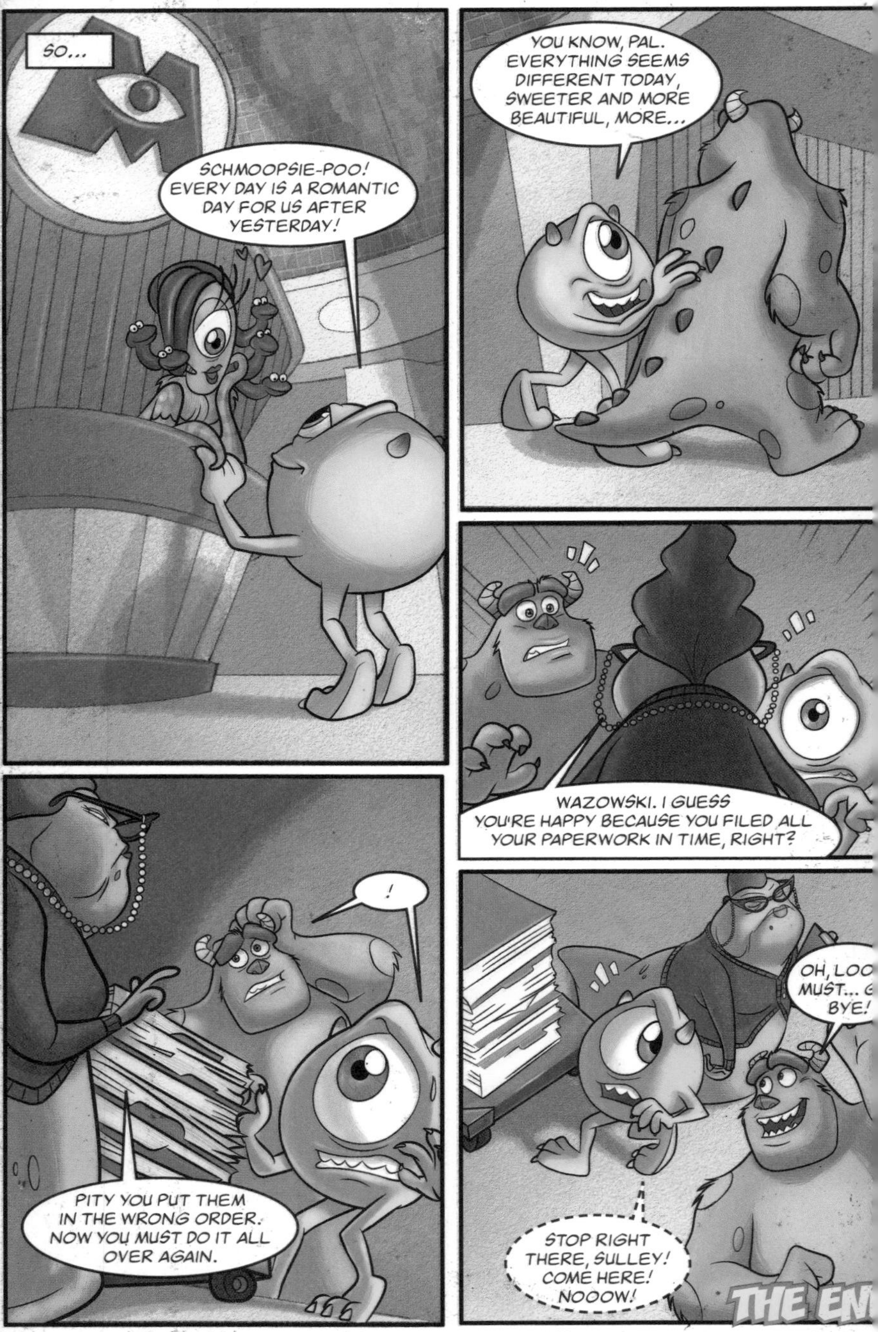
SO...
SCHMOOPSIE-POO! EVERY DAY IS A ROMANTIC DAY FOR US AFTER YESTERDAY!
YOU KNOW, PAL. EVERYTHING SEEMS DIFFERENT TODAY, SWEETER AND MORE BEAUTIFUL, MORE...
WAZOWSKI. I GUESS YOU'RE HAPPY BECAUSE YOU FILED ALL YOUR PAPERWORK IN TIME, RIGHT?
!
PITY YOU PUT THEM IN THE WRONG ORDER. NOW YOU MUST DO IT ALL OVER AGAIN.
STOP RIGHT THERE, SULLEY! COME HERE! NOOOW!
BYE!